Virginia Beautiful

THE NATURAL BRIDGE, ROCKBRIDGE COUNTY

Virginia Beautiful

By
WALLACE NUTTING

ILLUSTRATED BY THE AUTHOR WITH TWO HUNDRED AND
EIGHTY-FIVE PICTURES OF LANDSCAPES AND DWELLINGS

BONANZA BOOKS • NEW YORK

A WORD TO THE READER

WE ARE traveling together for a few pleasant hours to view beauty spots in old Virginia; not to read history.

We have recorded these beauties so far as the pages of this series on the States Beautiful will permit. Do not, therefore, throw down the volume with the exclamation, "Not a scene is recorded near my home!" One ought rather to be glad that Virginia is so rich in beauty that not even many hundreds of illustrations, compactly arranged, can more than cursorily touch the attractive regions of the state.

Especially in the matter of old houses Virginia could supply several volumes, so that our aim has been to exhibit as wide a variety of scenes as may be, distributed between landscape, stream, blossom, dwelling and mountain.

At least all these pictures are new, even if some show familiar outlines, and we venture that the majority of them depict subjects which have not before been shown.

The necessity imposed by weather conditions, or the leading of the highways, must account for an uneven treatment. It is the expectation of the writer, God willing, to follow this book by a companion volume, to contain notice of omitted sections, such as further journeys may disclose.

Meantime these illustrations are submitted, in the confidence that they are faithful to the subject in this very year of grace.

In all books on Virginia that the author has seen the text concerning old houses is largely taken up with stories of the people who lived in them, with slight reference to the date of the houses, and practically no reference at all to the peculiar merits of the architecture, or to the materials used. Now these latter matters are most important even to the amateur. Stories, however, are easy to obtain and under the plea of what is called "human interest," the omission of all technical details is cloaked. In the same manner the public has been compelled to be content with small and unclear pictures. In this work, therefore, the effort has been to supply pictures as large as may be since we cannot resist the impression that the public prefers a good picture with a narrow margin to a meager picture with a wide margin.

A WORD TO THE READER

The first idea in mind throughout has been to pack the book to the limit of its space with all the pictures possible.

The author thanks those residents who have opened their homes to him so graciously, and bespeaks the further courtesies of others who may offer to help him in what we seek to make a sympathetic and dignified and ample unfolding of old Virginia.

WALLACE NUTTING

Framingham, Massachusetts

THE CHARM OF VIRGINIA

IT MAY superficially appear odd that an alien to Virginian soil should take it upon himself to write about it. But my father is buried there, and for sixty-six years, mingling with her dust, he, who followed his duty as he saw it, as loyally as any Virginian could have done, has made the state a shrine for me.

The word shrine is much overdone, perhaps. The beginning of its use, confined to the graves of worthies, has been stretched by advertising to include too much. But no one regrets this more than sensitive Virginians. It may be allowed to a Northerner to unlease his soul, to glow over the region containing so much beauty set in a history so teeming with stimulation.

Permit, then, a stranger to become a familiar friend to the sweet slopes of these green acres, the clustering groves of oak and locust that embower your homes and churches, the soft far atmospheres of your lowland plantations, the broken mirrors of your streams outlined by frames of richer grace than Chippendale shaped, the tumbling wealth of your myriad hills, covered with pastoral peace, all backed by the charm of your ever mysterious mountains.

I, too, would contribute some small spray of honor to a region already rich in the tributes of so many more worthy appreciators.

History, romance, nature, these make Virginia attractive.

The people of Virginia are the living solvent through which all her other attractions are felt. The one word most descriptive of the people is kindliness. They are a proud people, yes, but their pride is not offensively obtrusive, because it depends on worth while things. In the two or three instances during our journeyings in Virginia, if the slightest hardening of manner was noticeable, the people who showed it were not Virginian born.

The owners of the old estates are increasingly being bored by the sightseers going the rounds. One wonders so much patience is shown, especially since lack of discernment may cause admiration for what is least admirable while the rarer and nobler aspects of the old life are not recognized.

VIRGINIA BEAUTIFUL

Be that as it may, Virginia is becoming the best known state to travelers, with the possible exception of California.

Washington, a city visited by a prodigious multitude, inhabited by the largest number of distinguished persons with the mood of travel, has become a source of Virginian tourists of almost unbelievable dimensions. Something approaching a hundred thousand persons will visit the Piedmont section this year to see the home of Jefferson, not to mention those who will go to that region for other reasons.

A state having within its borders the triple loadstones of Jamestown, Yorktown, and Williamsburg achieves, at once, uniqueness.

But Mount Vernon and Arlington, shrines of unnumbered pilgrims, the matchless Shenandoah, the numerous crystal caves ("one under every hill"), the magnificence of fertile farm lands, the great army and navy posts, the teeming commerce of Richmond and Norfolk, these have their appeals to one individual or another, till one may say Virginia sits securely by her sea and mountains, certain of capturing the admiration of all American generations. Her natural attractions are not as magnificent as those of California, and only fulsome and uncritical praise could make the claim. Her roadsides are by no means as generally bordered by pleasant habitations as is the case with some other states. The sea beaches are not found in conjunction with bold backgrounds. But take her for all in all, there is no state so rich in so much of interest; no state more stimulating to thought, or better worth investigating; no state which can vie with her in the number and beauty of her rolling expanses of rich countryside with the possible exceptions of New York and Pennsylvania, and no state with so large a portion of native people with such a natural basis as their background. Some other southern states have a still more undiluted American ancestry, but they are less developed than Virginia.

We may readily understand why state loyalty has grown so easily in Virginia. There is perhaps nothing comparable with it elsewhere in America except on the Pacific coast, where of course it has small root in heredity. The Virginian quietly takes it for granted that he lives in the best part of America. So far is this true that he feels proof superfluous and argument unnecessary, and but little acquaintance with Virginian backgrounds is required to understand this attitude.

A gentleman of Seven Oaks called me to note the names of the great oaks on his lawn. He had called them after the presidents, most of whom had lived in the county, others of whom had been connected with it by

CLOUD GHOSTS

A VIRGINIA GATE   A PLEASANT DETOUR

BLOSSOM KNOLL

UPPER BRANDON HALL TUCKAHOE GREAT HALL DOOR

THE RIVER DOOR, TUCKAHOE

YORK HALL

MONTPELIER

A VIRGINIA LAWN, BRANDON

property ties, long visitation, or family kin. Besides that, the lawn was beautiful. The oaks towered to unbelievable heights and their massive boles conveyed an irresistible impression of solidity and natural fellowship with the people below them. Facing all was a large, dignified, hospitable house inhabited by gracious people of culture. Under such environment it would be a strangely obtuse person whose roots did not spread in a soil so inviting, so rich in history, so beautiful, so eminently conducive to produce the fine flower of enriched manhood. Of course the very same surroundings may tolerate a diabolic nature, but such a home in Virginia seems to cry out to its children: "I have done all I could for you, all any country could do for you. Now, grow up!" And the best products are every inch men.

COPPERPLATE #30 RAWLINSON COLLECTION BODLEIAN LIBRARY OXFORD ENGLAND

ON THE following page is a print from original copperplate found in Bodleian Library, Oxford, England, by research worker engaged in securing information for restoration of colonial Williamsburg, Virginia. Restoration and research sponsored by Mr. John D. Rockefeller, Jr. Plate said to be most important discovery of American architectural research.

Plate shows: Upper panel: Left: Brafferton Indian School, College of William and Mary, erected 1723, first Indian School in America; *center,* front view of main building of College of William and Mary, erected 1695, and said to be the only example in America of work of Sir Christopher Wren; *right,* the President's House of the College of William and Mary, erected 1732, home of all presidents of America's second college and headquarters of Lord Cornwallis prior to Yorktown siege.

Center panel: Left: First Capitol building, known as such, in America, erected at Williamsburg in 1705 and burned in 1746; *center,* rear view of main building of College of William and Mary,—showing Chapel wing as erected in 1732; *right,* Royal Governor's Palace, erected at Williamsburg about 1705, home of royal Virginia Governors from that time to Revolution, and destroyed by fire 1781.

Lower panel: Illustrations of Virginia flora and fauna at time plate was made.

VIRGINIA BEAUTIFUL

The author is indebted to those who are restoring Williamsburg for this highly valuable plate, through the immediate agency of the Rev. Dr. A. R. Goodwin of Williamsburg.

It would be a matter of filling this volume if all the Williamsburg restorations were to be shown. It is probably sufficient to illustrate some of the most outstanding examples, in addition to the remarkable cut here loaned.

COLOR IN VIRGINIA

THE gorgeous red clay of Virginia is the most striking feature of color. In places where the roads have been cut through the hills, the effect is almost trying to the eyes, it is so brilliantly, and so extensively, and uniformly red. A great part of many of the counties is composed of this wonderfully colored soil. How beautiful it is and how effective appears at once when we happen to pass into a region of blue or white clay which becomes at once dreary. There is a warmth about this rich color so that a plantation formed of it has in spring either rich greens, or rich reds over the entire surface. Is it iron, which gives this effect? When the delicate evergreens begin to send out their new shoots, when the great leaves of the sycamore spread over the spring brooks, the poplar and the young pale oak leaves appear with all the other harbingers of the season, such a medley of green above the patches of red!

There are those who object to yellow color in the streams, but it does not bother me at all. It adds one more tint, striping the landscapes. Of course there are streams in other soils which are clear, and reflect shades of the arch above.

We have elsewhere mentioned the glory of the color that arises from the blossoms of the numerous flowering trees in Virginia. Probably the most superb effect, however, of color is that of a ripened grain field. Poets have done their best in describing it, and that best is never good enough. The corn, also, has a beauty in all its stages of growth, whether in summer or autumn, and the tobacco fields with their strong green, touched with olive, add their note. All told, the earth beneath the varied skies, and the tints that rush up the mountains, crowd the entire range of vision until there is nothing left to be imagined or desired. Even the russet of the early autumn, which indicates the rest of natural forces, has a mellowness and charm, for all things are beautiful in their time, and something is beautiful all the time.

THE BLOCK HOUSE

TO WHAT extent these fort houses were built we can form only a vague estimate. Some of them still exist in Maine. Possibly there are original examples in Virginia, but that at Crab Orchard is frankly a new erection in the old style, that this generation may know the measures the pioneers took for their defence (page 196).

In fort erection there was a quite general provision of a stockade, made of logs set upright and with pointed tips. The stockade was at some distance from the building or buildings of which it formed the outwork. Into the space behind the stockade the flocks, herds and wagons were driven, when attack was anticipated. We are reminded of the stone towers erected in many parts of western Europe, with space in the lower story to shield the cattle. It was found abroad that more room for that purpose was required, hence the outworks of castles.

The simple timber constructions like that described, afforded by their overhang a means of protection against an incendiary, since no one could safely approach the fort, being exposed to a direct plunging fire. But one wonders in this restoration, at the entire absence of loop holes.

The site is the Crab Orchard, in western Virginia.

It should be said that sometimes those block houses were not surrounded by palisades, and also we should recall that many of the dwellings were called garrison houses, being of brick, with solid shutters and great double oak doors.

Elsewhere reference is made to the construction of passages from the cellars of houses as retreats to subordinate buildings or to outlets on river banks.

In one way or another all dwellings were for fifty years or so subject to molestation, a thought suggested by the name Bacon's Castle. Washington and other officers erected wooden forts on the frontiers.

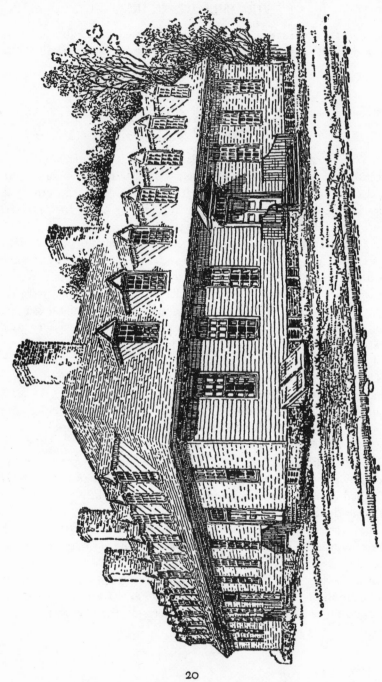

THE OLD INN OF WILLIAMSBURG

THE beautiful restoration here was important partly because Williamsburg needed a hotel. What more delightful than the bringing back of
the early atmosphere in a modern inn? This house in particular is unique
in the quaint extent of its low range of dormers and its general architectural
effect, and also because more than any other inn in America, perhaps in the
world, it has been a gathering place for important political and social events.
Here Henry and his confreres instituted the committee of safety. Here the
leaders of the Revolution met in conference. And here the first Greek
letter society is said to have been formed by students from neighboring
William and Mary College.

Before that time it was the scene of the state dinners given by the royal
governors. Patronized or pillaged by the soldiers of both sides in three
wars, it stands at length one of the finest pieces of work done under the
Rockefeller restoration of Williamsburg.

An old inn perhaps has more interest even than an ancient private
dwelling. For at the inn, especially here, we tread the very spot where the
life of the past streamed through—scholar, soldier, statesman, dowager,
matron and belle, adventurers and unknown persons of merit, all have left
an atmosphere behind them. It is a place for us all to come to, peculiar in
its interest and charm. Of course however many of these old buildings are
liable to destruction by fire.

In this volume we have in three or four instances sought to show old
houses as they were rather than as they are. The movement for restoration
is on us with a rush in Virginia. It has already destroyed much instead of
restoring, or added much that never existed.

So long as the self-conceit is rife which is trying to improve on the
eighteenth century we shall have a battle to fight in behalf of good design.

CONSTRUCTION OF HOUSES AND FURNITURE

A GOOD deal of misapprehension arises about the construction of good
houses and furniture. Owners exhibit almost with hushed breath,
the pinned frames of houses as if the pins showed the dwelling to be of great

age. All mortised frames were pinned, well into the nineteenth century indeed, until the balloon frame became the rule. Barns are built to this day, the frames of which are fastened together with great wooden pins, as it is the logical and proper way to fasten them. It is not done to save the cost of iron.

Similarly, furniture was quite generally pinned together within the memory of men now living, for the same reason. But even in the 1600's the drawer bottoms were often nailed on, and sometimes the heavy moldings on oak furniture.

The only point to guard against is turned pins which were never used, up to a very few years ago. Nails were not specially expensive in this country, more than in England. The cost of iron is of course less to-day than formerly. But iron was exported to England from Virginia, in the eighteenth century, in small quantities it is true; but if at all it was proof it was worth as much in England as here. The writer once having occasion for many wrought nails trained a boy to make them. He eventually provided six hundred "six penny" nails a day—a proof that the iron cost perhaps more than the labor, as it certainly did in the old time.

But of course old nails were saved, especially if the saving could be done by boys who were not otherwise earning anything. Many a time have I been set to picking nails out of wood ashes or extracting them from used lumber.

If nails were dear why were they used throughout the lathing? Of course the reason is that in this position they were covered.

Cultivation through Association

The cultivation of a taste for orderly, beautiful, harmonized physical things is scarcely attempted in the schools. Those who love art, to make a profession of it, are a very small proportion of the people. The purpose of every lover of the race should be to call attention always and everywhere to whatever is admirable because only so will the mass of men come to recognize it. One can, unhappily, find districts in every state where incongruity and unsightliness prevail, and it would seem that nobody within ten miles ever heard of beauty. Poverty in country regions is alleged as a reason for this condition. To a certain degree poverty is to blame. But that reason is by no means general. Ugly edifices of large cost are as common as dirt. The general public throughout America needs steady urgency to bring it to feel that ugliness is unnecessary, and therefore it is always a disgrace.

COZY GLADE COTTAGE   THE SIDE DOOR PATH

THE MONARCH OF WESTOVER

A LAUREL BANK

THE GREAT PECAN

GARDEN SHADOWS

A RIVER PATH

AN IVIED HOMESTEAD

THE DIVIDED PATH

VIRGINIA BEAUTIFUL

We hear of mothers who are always planning to bring their little children into contact continually with beautiful aspects of nature, and with tasteful fabrications of man, in the fond hope that the love of propriety in form may blend with the idea of moral grace. Is this merely a fond hope? Some enthusiasts claim that all children can be taught to sing. But we should dislike to hear the music some of them would make, even when doing their best. Similarly one doubts that all men have enough of the esthetic nature to know good from bad, in shape and color. Seeing the fashions in clothing, in furniture, in buildings, it is clear that one of the last things to make an impression is excellence in shape, and a sense of taste in the combinations of things.

But after these exceptions, there are millions who have had small leisure for admiring the excellencies of the world and who are delighted to have any discoveries of others disclosed to them. Their love for beauty grows by seeing it.

The contagion of taste, or at least that which arises from the imitative instinct, is plainly seen on streets and even in countries.

SHIRLEY-ON-THE-JAMES

THE date of this beautiful house (page 36) and even its builder are matters that are not fully settled, but considered on general principles paneling is not regarded as likely to date in America, much if any before 1700.

The external outstanding features of this house are its great height in proportion to its other dimensions, its rows of numerous dormer windows on every side, and its chimneys with their beautifully molded tops. It is obvious that the builder desired to have all sides of the master's house open to the light and without the obstruction of any subordinate buildings. In this particular he was very careful to set the large and handsome service buildings (page 30) not only back of the main front but many feet removed even, from the land entrance. One of the service buildings is shown. The other one is of the same size and symmetrically placed upon the grounds. These buildings being of two stories as they could be from their location, afford ample quarters.

The house interior is the most interesting in its panel work of any that the author has seen in America. The famous boxed stair, built on the well known architectural plan which gives it the air of standing alone without support, the number of the completely paneled rooms, the beauty of the detail over the room doors, each varying from every other, make the house an architectural gem of the first importance.

The impressive number and merit of the ancestral portraits, finding their perfect setting in these beautiful rooms, are crowning features.

The arrangement of the luxuriant trees (page 204) on the water front is not the set order so usual, and it is probable that the growth is somewhat more solid than was originally intended. Nevertheless there is an opening whose frame is the drapery of several trees of remarkably artistic shapes. The garden is on the down river side.

THE TOE OF VIRGINIA

THERE are no centers of considerable populations southwest of Roanoke with the exception of Bristol, which straddles over the Tennessee line, and is the nucleus of a large and beautifully diversified territory. Probably by the time these words greet the reader an alternate touring route will be completed from Bristol into the remote west of Virginia. We went down by Abingdon, Appalachia, Pennington Gap and Jonesville to Cumberland Gap, an unforgettable winding and twisting past mountain outwork, river bank, highland valley and the passes, each open to a more delectable world than that just passed.

Of course this route, reaching on to Kentucky and Tennessee is certain to be much followed. Hitherto access has been too difficult. But now no one could think of a more glorious location for a mountain home, accessible in a very few hours to large centers. We have in mind several valleys shown in these pages unsurpassed as sites. Americans have been a bit slow to avail themselves of the best in their country. Occasionally as about Asheville, farther south, it has been done. But here are a score of Ashevilles, visible to the eye of a very unimaginative person.

Temple mountain, what a fulcrum of power, what an array of beauty! All up and down from St. Paul, Pennington Gap, Gate City there is a series of contours comprising every known line of beauty and many others that have never been plotted by a human draftsman.

A FOREST OAK

AN OLD FORD

CLAREMONT GARDEN FRONT

THE GARDEN CORNER

The principal flowering trees are the locust and the dogwood, each in its own time, so that there is a long succession in the decorations of the fair slopes.   Evergreens, just being discovered as the best decoration for lawns, exist here in the hidden hills, forests in all their amazing conical perfection, and every twig tipped with its paler spring green.   Certainly mountains not too high to be clothed by forests are more attractive than bare heights. It was at Powell's and Holston rivers that we found our most perfect riparian compositions.   But Clinch River never reaches the limit of the complete pictures it can furnish; New River demands its share of admiration, till the traveler ends his days after reveling in new aspects of green and blue and white, and dreams of a succession of lovely images like the vision of new paradises.

At the summit of Cumberland Gap we reach a choice between west and southwest.   We are in full view of Middlesboro, in Kentucky, of Cumberland, in Tennessee, and of the highest mountain in Kentucky.   If we look east there are the many natural parks through which we have been winding.

A private road has been opened from the gap to a crest above it from which vast areas may be observed.   It is a region to be visited more than once.   With reluctance we turn back from this spot so rich in romance, where the pioneer, toiling westward through the wilderness, satiated his vision with the rich forest clad realm of Kentucky, the state founded in blood, and existing as poetry.   Here passed and repassed the rifle bearing, deerskin clad emissaries of the America that was to be.   They came because it was a country wonderful in worth and beauty, the newer Virginia, which long kept its political and ever retained its social ties with the Old Dominion.   The place names, the people, the customs of Kentucky and largely of Tennessee are only an extension of Virginia.   One who is at home in one of these states will be so in another.   They are one people, with one purpose, one history.   Virginia resigned her children, as they grew lustily, to become co-members in the national group, but no legislative act can change the blood, the customs, the affections of the people.   By giving them their freedom Virginia kept their love.

The science of this age, called into the service of brotherhood, has made an easy quick rolling way over gentle grades, and transportation binds these people into larger and more hopeful units.   The coming of a great through road is almost a redemption for those who, hidden before in painful tedious paths, were out of touch with larger mankind, but now are at the very front door of a nation.   If these mountain people will they may keep all that they had which was good and add, like a new life, the best that the world at large has to offer them.

The toe of Virginia seems rich with natural wealth, as it unquestionably is rich in the springing lines, the countless trees, the mounting scale of colors inherent in her landscape. There is room now that the road has come, and come so generously, for the world at large to tread the ways of these hills, and for those few who dwell there to avail themselves of this surprising opening, once unlooked for, to the broader outlooks.

The generation before us is certain to see a development of this southwest Virginia far fuller than all past ages have permitted.

A FREDERICKSBURG COTTAGE

THERE is at present a sign on this old cottage, which claims it as the birthplace of Monroe. We do not find, however, that this claim is endorsed by all students of the matter.

Aside from that question the dwelling is a pleasing example of the small country manor built in a town. This drawing seeks to give the old house as it was before the chimneys were lifted.

The design of the house is unique in the writer's observation. The showing of miniature gables projecting above the wing roofs is seen occasionally in houses of two stories. The total effect might well attract those who design the modern and unattractive bungalow. That these wings were original is proved by the chimneys. We think that someone here hit upon a wonderful design for a house of one story. It has character and considerable dignity, despite its humble dimensions. Ventilation could be secured at the little gables. When one sees with regret so many boxy houses in the country districts, of the South, built often with only a single room on another, and with a low pitched roof, the whole a sad blot on an otherwise pleasing landscape, it is well worth while to spread as widely as maybe some simple elements for design.

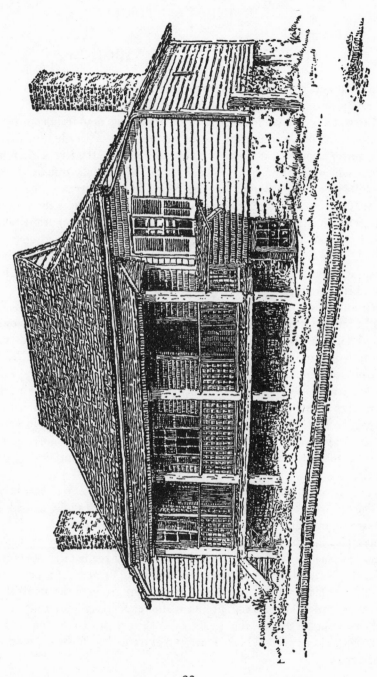

THE GEOGRAPHY OF VIRGINIA

ABRUPT and sharp demarcations, so loved by the pedantic mind, are really untrue of geography, and of most other sciences.

Tidewater Virginia blends so gradually with the mountain country that one passes out of the one into the other unaware of the line of division, for the very reason that it does not exist. To be sure the rivers often break into falls which definitedly mark the limit of Tidewater. But the contours of the hills throw out voluminous skirt trains, in easy curves at the outward edges. Nature tends to gentle outlines. It is mostly where the new roads cut deep wounds in mountain sides that the suddenness of transition obtrudes itself. When this occurs in rock formations the clean contrast is pleasing. But the long gravel or loam slopes we may trust will in time be covered, for safety and beauty, with some sort of vegetation capable of making good its hold and garlanding the grades.

Virginia lies in a shoe shape, its heel against the Atlantic, its toe insinuated between Tennessee and Kentucky. A flat southern sole line of some hundreds of miles is the base. West Virginia is on the instep and the top opens to Maryland.

Much of its eastern portions has been made by its rivers, and its lowlands are reminiscent of the east of England and must have reminded the settlers of the mother land. Barring the drainage of its vast western valley northeast to the Potomac, and portions of the southwest into North Carolina, the impression of the traveler is correct that the main rivers, the Potomac, the Rappahannock and the James move southeast into the Atlantic.

And historically it is on these streams that Virginia as we know it began.

The ships of colonial days with their moderate draught passed easily up these streams, and the York River, which is a great estuary. There was nowhere else in America except on the Delaware a region so conveniently laid out for the settler. The rivers were the only roads of importance.

Each planter selects a slightly rising ground, or at least a dry meadow as the site of his residence. In front of his own grounds the small ships of those days loaded his tobacco, grain or lumber for England, and almost to his door brought thence the stuffs or furniture which he had ordered. There was a closer personal relationship maintained with the old world than in the north.

A GARDEN LANE, UPPER BRANDON

A PATH AMONG BLOSSOMS

ROSES AT TALLWOOD

A SHIRLEY PATH

VIRGINIA BEAUTIFUL

The planter sent his sons, or at least the eldest, to England for his education, and for the continental tour to make that son, according to the estimate of those days, a finished gentleman.

The mechanic class was smaller than in the north, and as a consequence the energies of the settlers were directed to the land, while, except for building, manufactures were likely to be imported.

One reads with astonishment the list of immigrants, for, classified as they were, the number entered as gentlemen was often as large as the number of laborers or artisans. Shrewd Captain John Smith indeed says that some came as gentlemen who had not been so classed in England. But at any rate their status, announced by themselves, indicated that they did not expect to take hold with their hands, except of a sword, a bridle rein, or a glass.

The exigencies of a new land supplied a weeding out process. The reckless, the dissolute, the idle, either perished or reformed, and Smith admits that some of them became valuable citizens.

Meantime, as always, the character of the leading men, who by their courage, their wisdom or their property came to the fore, dominated the new communities at length, and supplied the tone and trend of the colony.

We are not chiefly, nor indeed secondarily concerned here with the history of Virginia. Our title calls only for attention to the aspects of beauty that present themselves in the Old Dominion, for these aspects, we are bold enough to say, deserve larger place than has been granted them in any treatment of Virginia. It is for this reason that the most historic spots are seldom shown by us, unless, besides the glamour of a romantic past, they also have now an esthetic appeal.

The geography of the state of course directs one to the sorts of scenes that one may love best.

At first thought it might appear that the lowlands would offer few attractions in their landscapes. But one could as well say Holland could not furnish material for her artists. The contours of the indented river shores, with their frequent fringe of trees, offer endless compositions capable of arresting the attention of every outdoor man. The moods of water surfaces, playing with the winds, the varieties of the foliage beckoning to the waters as elusively and as charmingly as a finished coquette, the paths through the woodland, the evening and morning lights across the waters as seen from the lawns that front the river estates are a few, and but a few, of the winning aspects of the tidal streams.

Beyond Norfolk and on the lower shores of the Chesapeake are broad beaches which lack none of those allurements of the ocean at play.

Persons from farther south find in summer an exhilaration at the ocean resorts, so that one is surprised to learn that the warmer, not the cold months are marked by the larger number of visitors.

The sea islands off the eastern shore and off the main coast have their votaries who cannot by any inducements of upland or mountain be drawn away from their favorite haunts. The breadth of nature's appeal is a constant marvel. What does not win upon one enthralls another. There is still enough of the primitive in men to love the border of the ocean where indeed life is thought to have begun. Certainly cruising among the salt channels offers tonic, sport, and the delight in uncertainty that is so human.

The mouth of Chesapeake Bay being in a central location on the Atlantic coast, contiguous to the national capital and many other great cities, and favored by a climate that renders winter drill practicable, is more and more becoming the center of naval activities. Norfolk and Newport News, being the outlet for a great coal and truck region, add to the importance of the mouth of the James.

VIRGINIAN CAVERNS

VIRGINIA, largely underlaid by limestone, offers in its broken country a perfect field for the formation of caverns and nature has not taken any time off in the carving she has done.

Up and down the Shenandoah, and on the eastern slopes of the Blue Ridge are almost as many caves as farms, and the advertisements of them are too much in evidence. The idea seems to be that the people "on the inside" make most of the money.

It is a fine farm that can be cultivated on the surface and bring in a revenue also on the underside. One wonders if cave hunting will ever cease. When caves become as common as blackberries perhaps their revenues will not be attractive.

The larger caverns are administered with a good deal of enterprise. The hotel or other sales place in connection is often over the mouth of the cave, which is shown by guides, and elaborately lighted. Color effects of much

NELSON HOUSE GARDEN   MONUMENTS AT JAMESTOWN

A GLOUCESTER FARMHOUSE

BENN'S CHURCH   ST. JOHN'S, RICHMOND

THE OLD DIGGES HOUSE, YORKTOWN

ABINGTON CHURCH

MARY WASHINGTON'S PARLOR

THE WILLOW OAK AND TODDSBURY

BRUTON CHURCH, WILLIAMSBURG

A ROSEHILL CURVE

PRESIDENT MONROE'S BOX   DRAWING ROOM DOOR, KEIM HOUSE

QUARTERS, SEVEN OAKS

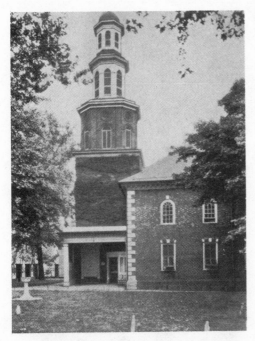

CHRIST CHURCH, ALEXANDRIA

STRATFORD SCHOOL

THE GOVERNOR'S MANSION

STRATFORD, WESTMORELAND

MIRADOR GARDEN ARCHES

MARY WASHINGTON'S BIRTHPLACE, EPPING FOREST

beauty are secured. The rough places have been smoothed, and the circuit is made agreeably enough.

Jefferson noted that the temperature of these caverns is uniform with one another and also throughout the year, about fifty-six degrees.

It is curious to see certain mosses growing near the electric lights, which have come into being through the light, and are not found elsewhere.

The beauty of the calcareous formations is remarkable and perhaps not too highly praised. The fancy finds fine play in naming the shapes. Imagination always needs stimulation and the names we give objects reflect our culture, or the lack of it. It has been found worth while to call in experts to secure fine lighting effects. Every conceivable color presents itself. When we remember that marble is one form of limestone we may rightly expect that these fantastic curtains, these magnificent stalactites, these massive domes, moist from the seeping water, will present all the variations of multi-colored marbles. These houses, not built with hands, might easily have inspired Job or Shakespeare or Jules Verne to adorn their tales by a setting of marvel, grandeur, and mystery.

While the Indians had some limited knowledge of these caverns there is little evidence of their use by cave dwellers. It is natural for all life to love and seek the sun. The treasures hidden here are exhibited by the wizardry of geology and chemistry and not as discoveries of spoliations long past.

One speculates on the catacombs where early Christians made their abodes under and about Rome. Here no hand need be lifted to afford a refuge for multitudes, and the lofty arches of some great chambers have obviously suggested "the long drawn aisle and fretted vault" of the cathedral.

We inquired what was the effect on the guides of continued stays under ground and learned that the only effect observable was a slight oppression of the heart. The depths are confined to a very few hundred feet. One feels no fear or sense of depression. Yet after a long tour the sweet day is welcome. After all we are surface animals. The writer has elsewhere called attention to the fact that very few people live in forests. The desert itself is more populous. The tribes especially addicted to forests are the pigmies. Nor does bird life find its chosen home away from the sun.

The age of the caverns is of course immense and computations of the rate of incrustation bear out fully the aeon spaces claimed by geology. It is a world so old that we live in! Much of its beauty depends on its age. When and if it lasts long enough however to bring down all its mountains into a plain much of the charm of life will disappear. We need variety as a stimulus and happily we are likely to have it for an indefinitely long time.

SIMPLE OLD FREDERICKSBURG HOUSES

ON THE river street, mingled with various old warehouses, are also charming little dwellings with quaint stoops. No liberties have been taken in the drawing except to replace the shingles on one roof.

The importance of ports is shifting owing to the deeper draft of modern ships. Formerly the limits of tidewater here, and at Petersburg and at

Richmond and Georgetown, on the principal rivers of Virginia, were the transfer points for freights going into the upper South Side, the Piedmont and the Valley, and even beyond. Towns always spring up at such points, for warehouses and trading. Fredericksburg was convenient for much of the back country. Another feature of interest here is the landing place of the ferry where George, escorting Betty Washington, crossed daily to school. For the Washington farm was on the other side. Fredericksburg is more and more becoming important as a center of old sites, for the boyhood home

A MANTEL AT KENMORE

COTTAGE CORNER, SHENANDOAH VALLEY

WARE CHURCH

THE END OF THE PATH

OLD ACCOMAC, DEBTOR'S PRISON

is that where the character is formed. Washington was always more at home in and about Fredericksburg than anywhere else except Mt. Vernon.

Fredericksburg is also the first point going south where one may swing southeast to the northern and other necks. While it has always been a small city it has ever been a center of a good society and the location of many good homes. Perhaps to-day it is one of the three natural headquarters for the study and enjoyment of Virginia, owing to the number and quality of its old dwellings.

THE PICTURES IN DETAIL

A VIRGINIA Gate (page 12) is an entrance off Cary Road not far from Richmond. As the gate of an estate is in a manner an introduction to what is behind it, and as first impressions count heavily it has been felt through all the ages that a handsome or an imposing gate was important.

Still opinions may differ as to the question whether an entrance should be made up of natural or artificial features, or a blending of the two. Fine trees almost form a portal in themselves. When such trees flank a gateway the artificial, or architectural features, if any, can be more readily subordinated as here.

The most attractive gate in the author's memory was one vast tree, whose magnificent limb reached above the drive, the outer side of the entrance being outlined by a handsome shrub.

A Pleasant Detour (page 12) from the way south over the Lincoln highway, near Pulaski, took one past several cuttings through a cliff, over which foliage had spread. In time all bare walls of the new road will decorate themselves.

Blossom Knoll (page 12) seen on the route from Ashland to Orange is one of those charming small houses, which perhaps escapes the notoriety of a name, but which is not less attractive on that account. Set between the blossoms, on a gentle elevation, with one chimney covered by vines; with dormers and porch, it is just as good in outline as if it were very exclusive. These are the homes where the youth of America are growing up with some feeling of beauty, inevitable from their surroundings.

An Old Ford (page 29) reminds us that in the early days there were no bridges, but only ferries for large streams and fords for the brooks.

An occasional awkward situation arose in a time of flood. Then it was that the pioneers must swim their horses. They kept their heads above water better than the modern motors.

This little old house in Fredericksburg is the home of Mr. P. V. Daniel. The owner has a copy of a deed from the court house showing that George Washington bought it from Fielding Lewis, the first of June, 1761. It is said that this deed is signed by Washington himself, and not by his business manager as most, if not all of the others, are. The house is peculiar in having two chimneys so near together on one end. It would indicate that the owners made no attempt to heat the other end of the house.

The Monroe law offices in Fredericksburg are open as a kind of museum. They do not mark any particular architectural style, being a simple one-story roof.

The monument to Martha Washington was dedicated by President Andrew Jackson with much ceremony.

The monument to Dr. Hugh Mercer in the attractive open common, and the apothecary's shop which he conducted are also shown.

THE AGE OF DWELLINGS

THERE is very little documentary proof of the age of old houses in Virginia, or anywhere else for that matter. The age of a dwelling or piece of furniture is determined by the object itself, its style, chimneys, moldings, framing and many little items which taken together are convincing.

There is a Virginian house, regarding which the state has placed a legend, by the roadside, dating it in the 1600's. Its restoration is there said to be just before the Revolution, for a brick in the chimney bears the date, baked in, as of the 1770's. Now the chimney is usually the oldest because the most solid part of a house. That both the identical chimneys in this house should be restorations and that all the sash, molding, mantels, and in fact all parts that can be examined should be of the later date raises the strong presumption that the entire house replaces an earlier and cruder dwelling.

Documents are perhaps found indicating that a house was built on a plantation at a certain date. It is always an unwarranted assumption that the dwelling mentioned is the one now standing, unless it is itself a monument of the methods of that age.

It is quite clear that in the early seventeenth century the country was too new to boast many fine dwellings. We find few claims are made for that century; but even if made for eighteenth century styles, to be of that century the style must back the claim.

There was a considerable spreading abroad of populations by 1660. By 1690 we find much evidence of wealth, and from that time on, but mostly after that time, the great houses rose.

One almost sure sign of age is the fenestration. Windows with broad muntins were universal until late in the eighteenth century. If the muntins at Kenmore at Fredericksburg were original they would be proof that the house is not as old as it is claimed to be. But too much is known of this famous dwelling to place it later than its recorded date, the middle of the eighteenth century. Hence we know the window sash is a replacement. I would undertake to find a hundred houses in Virginia of the date of Kenmore, all with broad muntins, that bear all marks of age. Hence muntins in fine condition of a lighter sort are easily classed as replacements.

THE RESTORATION OF VIRGINIAN HOUSES

HERE, as elsewhere, how many crimes are committed in the name of restoration! Of course the purpose of restoration, at least if the purpose is reasonable, is to bring back the effects of the original. If then a complacent owner explains how he thought he would like this room larger, or that window moved, or this new fireplace or new porch obviously what he gets is a mongrel. It is neither one thing nor another. An entirely new house may be made in good taste. A very old house may be restored in good taste. But it is never good taste to make improvements; with the solitary exception of the plumbing necessary which may usurp small old rooms, but neither partition, chimney, window, doorstep, mold, stair should be changed a hair. There is a passion, which has spread like measles, not to use so harsh a word as the plague, for buying and "fixing up" old houses. Many persons get their principal joy in life out of this proceeding. If the architect whom they employ is not amenable to persuasion, they get another. As architects need work they often honestly persuade themselves they do no wrong by yielding to the whim of their clients. Architects need a close trade union!

A fine old Virginian house comes to my mind which has not only had most of its roof lines changed, but its size, style, finish—in fact everything that gave it merit. Well, what are we to do? The offenders cannot be sent to jail, and ostracism is out of date. That is why we let the bad work go on. For these instances are not isolated. They are, in milder degree, the rule rather than the exception. The most notable two (allow the phrase) houses in Virginia have had wings added radically different from the original. They dwarf the main house. Why multiply instances? A generation ago these things might have been overlooked but now all men ought to repent. As if it were not enough to ruin the dwelling, the furniture also violates the period of the house. At Mount Vernon there are some examples which had no existence in Washington's day, a condition without excuse, if it is true that approximately a half million paying visitors a year visit it.

I call to mind, however, various worse examples. One house contains in a single room oak, walnut, mahogany, pine, maple furniture. It is good, restored, or spurious. It is English, American, French, Canadian. It is Northern and Southern. It ranges from the daintiest lightest examples to the crude products fit only for a cabin kitchen. It is without arrangement, purposely. But early furniture was always arranged in rather particular

AN OLD SHOP, WILLIAMSBURG

BRANDON HALL

CHURCH RUINS, JAMESTOWN

CAPITOL AT RICHMOND

form. In short it is shown and gloried in, under the impression of the owners that it is attractive. While a few individual pieces may be good the total effect is bad, as the impression given is not that of a stately old room but of a shop where promiscuous furniture is sold.

An owner may say "I have not sought to furnish in period." But he has bought at least what he regards as antiques. If a jumble was not in good taste in the eighteenth century, it is not good taste now. Custom has nothing to do with taste. It may be custom to put oak and Windsors with mahogany, but the effect is never good. It does not remind one of the old days nor of present styles. It hurts the house, it fails of what great sums have been expended to secure—an atmosphere.

A Gloucester Farm House (page 39) represents another one of those places of which we are fond, although it does not appear among the famous estates shown in books of Virginia. We feel strongly that there are thousands of such places, worthy of admiration in themselves, and the boyhood homes of many who have been good citizens in every department of life. In fact while a name is attractive and a history is interesting neither means of necessity very much. It is the sort of character that develops in these old homes that counts, either in heaven or earth.

The Willow Oak (page 41) is a decorative tree which sometimes spreads abroad its massive proportions on the old river lawns of Virginia as at Toddsbury. The soil along the rivers seems capable of producing trees of almost any size. One great tree is impressive when we see it and in the retrospect of memory. Such trees seem to give a dignity to the men who foster them.

Toddsbury (page 41) is a very perfect house of moderate size, which has long appealed to those who visit Virginia. The porch with a room over is a probable addition though it has been in place many years. The hall is not a passage but a square room with a stair; it is used as was probably intended, as a living room. The old parlor has rarely good paneling. Every one of the rooms has character. The old box locks, and other hardware is, largely, in position.

The house is unusual in having a wing from one side and built to harmonize with the main house in height and otherwise. The genial Mott family, the owners for a generation, cherish their dainty old place.

A sweet pastoral glimpse along the river bank is shown (page 62).

The President Monroe (page 44) place near Charlottesville, recently acquired for restoration by Mr. Johns, is famous for its impressive growths of box, most advantageously seen as here from the balcony of the porch.

The rear of the house has developed, with the high basement, interesting early features well rewarding inspection. In time no doubt the front will be brought back to its original contours.

Mary Washington's Birthplace, (page 46) Epping Forest, gains the interest attaching to the early home of the mother of a celebrated man, because we are warranted not only by history but by biology in ascribing the characteristics of a man more largely to his mother than to his father. The mother of Washington, whose history is not a large page in literature, is known sufficiently to convince us that she possessed the sturdiest virtues and a highly independent nature. We are most fortunate in being able to have her birthplace here and her last residence at Fredericksburg preserved. Epping Forest has been reduced in extent and the house has its dormers removed. But lying as it does in a purely rural country, there is no reason why it may not ever continue the undisturbed relic of an earlier time. One of the subordinate structures, the ice house, is an ancient vast bricked pit, with an unusually picturesque roof.

Scalloped Paths (page 59) represents a portion of the Mt. Vernon gardens, which tradition says were laid out personally by Washington, and in a matter of this kind we may feel a good deal of assurance that the story is correct. Being a surveyor he would naturally lay out his own garden, though it is equally true no doubt that Martha stood near with suggestions. It is a spot, therefore, where we get close to the brightest side of the family. The residence itself has been so thoroughly made known by pictures everywhere that it seemed better here (page 87) to show the house from such an angle as to get its connection through its segmental curtain, with the dependencies. Of course the other end is similarly connected.

Mt. Vernon is said to be visited by about a half million people annually. In this respect it probably surpasses any spot in interest to Americans. Foreign travelers also, by courtesy or interest or both, go in great numbers, as its location is most happy for the convenience of visitors. The dwelling has been described so often that we only remark on the generally worthy character of the contents. The location could scarcely be more beautiful. It escapes the flat environment of the Tidewater estates. The lofty bluff on which it rests is impressive seen from the river, and the outlook from it is commanding, even superb.

Many who find themselves in Washington or thereabout on Sunday afternoons are sorry to learn that it is not then open. They consider a visit to the tomb of the Father of his country is an act closely akin to worship,

A TIDEWATER COURT HOUSE

SCALLOPED PATHS

ON THE SHENANDOAH

ROSE TREES

ACROSS THE BOXWOOD

MIRADOR ENTRANCE GATE

THE LAWN AT TODDSBURY

THE JAMES AT SHIRLEY

more so indeed than anything else people are likely to do. As to the petty sum charged for admission it is of course expended on the upkeep which is very large. Numerous caretakers are essential to guard against vandals.

Parnassus (page 75) is not a fanciful name supplied by the author, but is the true name of the town near by this pastoral scene.

The flocks of Virginia are still much in evidence, and, either in spring or fall are the greatest attractions of the state. The lambs lying here with their mothers carry our thought back quickly to the earliest racial experience.

There are three things we hope humanity will never forget. They are the three strongest impressions even now on man's memory. A glowing fireplace, rain on a low roof above a bed in the loft, and a flock of sheep with lambs. If we keep these three we shall never be anarchists, cynics or reprobates.

Rockhill (page 78) in Fauquier county, near Warrenton. Rockhill (emphatically without rocks or hills) is a plantation quite out of the ordinary. The main structure has on one side a recessed paved porch, rarely found, and beautifully shaded. On one side (page 217) a quite different aspect of a dormered range of rooms opens to us a pleasing approach. On another (page 25), as Garden Shadows, appears the walk leading to the main front. The Williams family have here a large, rambling, attractively furnished mansion, which (on proper introduction) they show with much graciousness. It is one of the most homelike abodes in Virginia, and yet it is totally without a set plan.

THE GADSBY TAVERN, ALEXANDRIA

A NORTHERN museum, I believe the Metropolitan, secured paneling in this historical and architecturally fine tavern, and we may hope that the multitudes who see that paneling in the metropolis will offset the loss to Alexandria. However the citizens were stirred up and a local organization has undertaken the restoration of this the best part of the tavern.

This hostelry was for Alexandria something like what the Raleigh Tavern was to Williamsburg. For here Washington and many leaders continued to come, as the populations pushed inland, and the travel was more westerly than easterly. To be sure the shift of the capital to Richmond from Wil-

liamsburg did not occur officially till late in Washington's life, but the trend was already strong. Alexandria, having unimpeded navigation of the Potomac, became the main port on the river. It was the nearest city to Mt. Vernon. It was the point where all traffic and visitation to the plantations southeast on the river and the northern neck began. Braddock's ill advised expedition started hence. And he, meeting Washington at this inn, made the young patriot his aid. To the very year, nay month of his death, Washington was called here, and he here enlisted and disbanded or bade farewell to his comrades, become veterans.

MYERS HOUSE PARLOR   KEIM HOUSE LIBRARY

THE AMPLITUDE OF WILLIAMSBURG

ANOTHER NATURAL BRIDGE

We are interested in the edifice because it proves how the almost sheer simplicity of its front acquired dignity under the magical fingers of the carpenter-architects of that time, who built better than we because they personally carried out their own designs. We have heard it said that it is now impossible to build in this way. I wonder.

The old saying about the sashes in houses of about 1760 was that they should be four lights wide and six high. It is possible that in the very finest houses they made a point of somewhat larger glass even in that period The author makes no attempt to vouch for the sizes shown in the Gadsby Tavern, but it seems extraordinary that these large windows should have originally had only twelve rather than twenty-four lights of glass. Neither do we know whether the cellar windows are now correct as one of them is set lower than the others.

POHICK CHURCH

AMONG the finer churches of the Old Dominion and celebrated as one of the two with which Washington was connected is Pohick, reached from Mt. Vernon by a much shorter road than that followed by the main highway. The Northern soldiers seemed very frequently to have chosen the churches as stabling quarters, but the fine restorations carried on here have obliterated, on the interior, the damage done, while the exterior was nearly intact. The fine quoins, doorheads and windows are noticeable and ivy has already begun its process of loving decoration. The date is 1769, following an edifice of wood.

The parish was already of respectable age in Washington's time and may be supposed contemporary with Mt. Vernon.

Washington is reported to have helped with or wholly furnished many drawings for his neighbors' houses and this church, though his work in this respect was not as extensive or ambitious as that of Jefferson, who had the advantage of European travel. Washington's work was designed to be utilitarian as became his emphatically practical nature.

One should understand however that metropolitan churches are not to be looked for except in metropolitan areas.

These Virginian churches which we are showing were, with the exception of Williamsburg and one or two others, chapels, so far as dimensions are

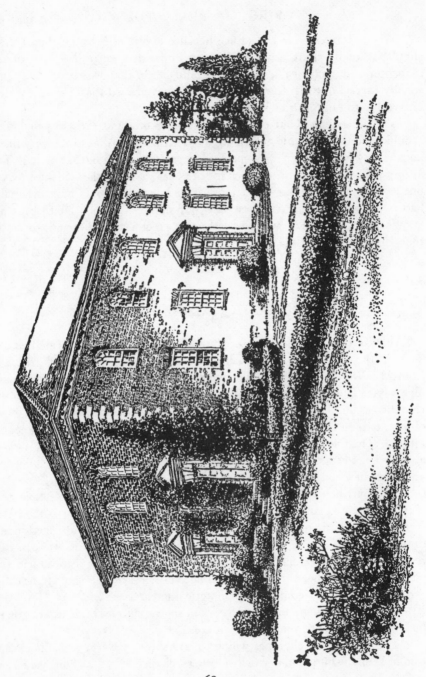

PATRICK HENRY'S KITCHEN   MORVEN FROM GARDEN

A CARY ROAD OAK

LONGBRANCH PASTURES

AN OLD HILL ROAD

THE MILL ROAD, CLARKE COUNTY

concerned, for the use of purely rural neighborhoods. But even so one notices an almost total departure from the models of the English village church, and an absence of ecclesiastical emphasis. Indeed that feature seems to have been common north and south among Church of England people as well as dissenters, and in both regions the edifices were often used for political gatherings.

FURNITURE IN VIRGINIA

VIRGINIA and the South in general for long have been the source of much fine mahogany. It is therefore with feelings of keen disappointment that one finds the shops filled with English and French frauds. They are the more dangerous because often the dealer is not conscious of selling spurious stuff. Persons in need of an income take kindly to selling what they suppose to be antiques. Good Virginian antiques are not any longer to be had at bargain prices. So the fraudulent pieces are forced up in proportion to the real. The credulous traveler, because he is in the Old Dominion, is deceived. That happens no less when the articles are frankly admitted to be foreign. The argument is that the planters imported their furniture, hence it is proper to do so now. The fact is overlooked that good pieces are as rare abroad as here. Of the supposedly old furniture from abroad not one in ten, to put it carefully within bounds, that I have seen, is real. Then upon this devoted state are also dumped out the products of various factories making alleged reproductions, with dowels instead of mortises, and from patterns skimped in design to avoid costs. In a word the whole matter is so redolent of ignorance, fraud, cheapness of design, and so without intelligent purpose in selection and assembling that any serious honest tourist is made sick at heart. Those old houses held by the old families, with their old furniture, are a refreshing retreat. It is a consolation to chat with persons who are not displaying with gusto the acquisitions which they boast of buying cheap, but which were dear, whatever the price.

Virginia is both blessed and cursed by being rediscovered. In instances persons of wealth and taste have come to the rescue of old plantation houses, and have become worthy adoptive children of Virginia. In other instances it would have been far better to let the dignified old places sink into mother earth.

THE GARDENS OF VIRGINIA

THIS particular garden is unusual in being shut in all about by town houses. Such surroundings impart an atmosphere of attractive seclusion like gardens of the orient. (Page 74)

The garden is found at the rear of the Edgar Allan Poe Memorial Stone House, and calls beckoningly to travelers to rest and refresh themselves here at leisure.

The gardens of Virginia have long been her pride. The owners of fine estates have pretty generally, with few exceptions, opened their gardens for a week in spring. The Garden Club has issued an attractive book descriptive of the gardens which are available for inspection.

The box borders of Virginia are a feature prized partly because the box grows here so beautifully, escaping winter kill, and partly because it seems the fashionable shrub. It has the distinguished merit of being attractive all the time—in which particular it is worthy of emulation.

The rose in Virginia is a spring rather than a summer flower. Where on some neglected quarters it has been allowed to run riot the effect of the all enveloping bloom is almost overpowering. Nowhere else have we had the experience of sweet garden odors coming to us on the highway as we drove along.

The perfume of the grape, which is rife in summer in Virginia, is a delicious memory.

It is more often necessary however, to enter the gardens, since they are connected with remote estates, and the garden front is not the street front, because the very idea of the garden was a place apart for the entertainment of friends. There was nothing of French publicity about the English families that settled Virginia.

When they appeared in public with coach and four that was a side of their character, but at home they retreated to be with friends. Gardens therefore may be behind high walls. They may be mingled with fruits or vegetables, where people follow the old fashions, and that again is another reason for seclusion. The cherry and pear and plum trees required, sometimes, a wall, because there were youthful marauders from of old. The formal garden was indeed a part of every estate which made any pretention to be fashionable. It was the time when in England garden parties and entertainments were the height of fashion.

Indeed the light Windsor chair, painted green, came into popularity first as a garden chair, before it was used in the dwelling. Hence the paint.

The French taste, so fully set forth in the old paintings of fops and belles in gardens, was partly responsible. But the Virginia climate, so much softer than the English, made doubly apt Tennyson's invitation "Come into the garden, Maud!" In fact, when the weather permitted, the garden came to be the usual resort for all leisure daytime hours. Hence so many summer houses, garden pavilions, temples, settees, under every inviting shade. Those places free from mosquitoes were therefore cherished. Curiously there were, on our last visit to Mt. Vernon, swarms of black flies, but down river at Wakefield the air was entirely clear of any insect, a paradise by the riverside. Perhaps the incident was a mere chance. It may be that water in gardens was less frequent because of its harboring insects. Certainly water, led about or in pools, is necessary to supply the crowning beauty of a garden, by its contrast, its reflections, its cooling effects and that loveliest aspect of nature, the meandering bank of a stream.

The Days of Yore (page 81). Some distance from Cary Road peeping out between screening trees, this old house, so appealing, so full of possibilities for restoration, appears to challenge us. It is one of those deceptive places, built on a gentle slope, so affording good basement rooms on the rear. Both chimneys, the length of the roof, and the front edge of the porch are vine covered. There is a cozy recessed porch at the back, fine old trees all about and "nobody home."

A good modern farmhouse beyond doubtless might house the person working the fields. Twice we passed delightful hours here, dreaming, scheming and sketching. What a joy to engage in making such a dear old house into a home!

An Eastern Shore Farm Road: This subject (page 82) is a favorite with the author because there is just enough humanity in it, not too much, and the rest is nature. A winding farm road bordered on the one side by cabbages, on the other side by great murmuring pines, three of them in a row decorated by columbine, gave us an ensemble of columns far superior to the architectural orders of the Greeks and Romans. They think of columbine in Virginia as a nuisance, there is so much of it. So might one feel I suppose, if he were obliged to walk over loose gold pieces as a highway!

Stratton, the ancient and excellent plantation house here, is thought by the state commissioners of highways to date in part from the seventeenth century. It is set where one approaches through avenues of trees. Its

73

kindly owner welcomes us. He dwells in the midst of vast potato fields, whose lavender blossoms, row on row, supply an entrancing color scheme.

It would not become us to enter into the rife debate on the question of the national government's assisting in the restoration of Williamsburg so far as exercising the right of eminent domain over those private estates yet remaining in the Duke of Gloucester street and elsewhere. One can understand that persons who have always lived in their old homes here may wish to continue to do so. Possibly an amicable arrangement could be entered into by which owners would agree to fall into line so that the upkeep of their properties would harmonize them with the restorations and so that in case of change of hands the government should have the first right of purchase.

THE EDGAR ALLAN POE SHRINE

THIS ancient stone house, called the oldest dwelling now standing in Richmond, but whether rightly or not I do not know, is at least a most interesting edifice. The interior is also worth observation. Of course shut-

ROANOKE VALLEY

THE HOME PASTURE

PARNASSUS

TERRACE OF STEPS

MORVEN KITCHEN

CHRIST'S CHURCH, LANCASTER

GARDEN FRONT, WESTOVER

ROCKHILL

INFORMALITY, WINDIEKNOWE

VIRGINIA HOUSE, RICHMOND

ESCAPE LODGE AND A LANE

LAWN, EPPING FOREST

NORTHUMBERLAND LAUREL

THE DAYS OF YORE, NEAR RICHMOND

ters, at the period of this house, were not used in the form shown, but were ordinarily solid. A warm climate, however, induced the settlers in Virginia to change that custom before many years, abandoning the early style as soon as it became safe. For shutters were primarily designed for protection against violence, not against sun heat.

This dwelling with another on the right at the rear is filled with memorials of Poe who resided not here but with the Allans. The garden directly back of this house has been tastefully designed. The contents of these memorials consist of such important and unusual pieces of furniture, besides many letters, papers, pictures, et cetera, that the student of Poe can profitably occupy himself here for a considerable period of time.

The location is in the old end of Richmond. The other private places in town are of interest largely in connection with the nineteenth century and while they are substantial residences have not the distinction in architecture which belongs to the earlier time, but historically are important. Some of great interest were burned in the war. It is, however, a matter of astonishment and congratulation that so many historical places escaped.

ST. JOHN'S CHURCH, HAMPTON

THIS famous ancient edifice has been subject to more or less change and demolition. It is represented to have had a tower and spire at one time, but we are entitled to presume that its restoration after the Civil War is on the original lines. To be sure the earliest churches, as those of Jamestown, and its apparent counterpart, Benn's Church near Smithfield, had towers, and so has Bruton Church. But the towerless cruciform Flemish brick church predominated, as a journey through Tidewater Virginia very impressively shows. These edifices are deceptive because their exteriors are kept to a modest, almost severe tone of decoration, but within they were elegant to a degree, with their handsomely wrought hooded pulpits and their great paneled pews.

It should be understood that these were the state churches, of the established faith, although they were sometimes donated entire by rich planters; sometimes the pews were bought outright without reference of course to the cost of the pew, but at a price proportioned, according to the cost of the church, among the planters of the parish. Also the parish system obtained as a political division as in England. Built in 1727, it is about all that is left of Old Hampton. The communion service dates back to 1617, though it is supposed first to have belonged to an earlier church. Its "breeches" Bible presented by Miss Lathers, and the Pocahontas window, by Indian students of Hampton, are of course recent acquisitions.

The fashion of using the weeping willow about churches and cemeteries and even on estates, without any connection with the idea of mourning was much favored. In those days people were not afraid to be near their dead, and to enlist nature in appropriate emblems for them. Silk pieces representing tombs and weeping willows were popular.

Hampton is an interesting city owing to its being the seat of the famous Institute, which is a monument to the wisdom and consecration of General Armstrong.

Climate

The difference between northern and southern climate, is not that the southern is hotter on any one day, but that there are more warm days in the south. Those who love the broad open plantations of central and southern Virginia will find them very tolerable as to temperature. They are parti-

cularly agreeable in the winter for those numerous persons who do not enjoy the debilitation that presses upon one farther south. For the lower country however we favor the Gloucester region or the Northern Neck. The southwestern slopes of the Blue Ridge are more tonic than the lowlands but are not so thoroughly continental in climate as the Valley. The Valley in its northern part is actually no farther south than Baltimore. Snows are common in the valley for some hundreds of miles, but they do not lie long except in the northern portion. For considerations of health and to encourage a sturdy physique one would say that anywhere on the slopes of the mountain ridges would be favorable.

The world was, intellectually and politically, during the classical period governed by races in the south temperate zone, but with the beginning of the middle ages and after, it has been ruled by men of the north temperate zone. It would seem therefore more to be a matter of organization or accident, that brings nations and regions to the fore. Even near the Equator there is a race of very large athletic men. The influence of the climate on races, within moderate limit, has probably been overestimated.

Mirador, the residence of the Tree family, at a moderate distance from Charlottesville, is particularly notable on account of its massive and beautiful entrance gates. These are so admirably designed for imposing effect and so daintily decorated with vines that they may be said to be preëminent in this respect. The garden also (pages 46 and 61) is well worth while. The estate is not generally open to the public, and we are not in a position to speak definitely in relation to its age. The effect however seen through the gate of the dwelling as one passes by, may be enjoyed by anyone.

THE CHARLOTTESVILLE REGION

WHOLLY distinct from the Tidewater region, not merely in location but in the character of its dwellings, is Charlottesville.

We may fairly attribute the choosing of this region to a peculiar soil. It is a long and narrow upland strip, all at a good elevation and marked by the pleasing peculiarity that on the very tops of its rounded slopes the fertility is as great as elsewhere. This circumstance is impressive as one looks out from Charlottesville at Monticello, itself on a lofty hill, and sees looming to the left of it a much higher hill beautifully cultivated.

WASHINGTON'S MOTHER'S ROOM   MORVEN MANTEL

MOUNT VERNON, FAIRFAX

MONTPELIER ARBOR AN OLD QUARTERS

VINE BOWER NEAR CLIFTON FORGE

VIRGINIA BEAUTIFUL

The district escapes the plain country at its eastern foot, and it is free of the rougher Blue Ridge region to the northwest. It seems marked out almost, as predestined, to the particular class of people who settled there. It is unlike any other part of Virginia.

Looking back we see that Virginia was settled at the worst point for the health of its people. The mosquitoes and bad water nearly killed the colony. In New England, the Pilgrims picked about the worst land that could be found for cultivation, but there was an abundant clear stream tumbling down from the hills.

The Piedmont has all the healthfulness of Plymouth and all the fertility of the Tidewater. Jamestown was malarial and even the water was brackish.

It required a long time for the lowlands to fill up so as to make the Piedmont safe for residence. But while the Tidewater soon became rich Plymouth was always poor. And Piedmont, its soil also singularly free from stones, became a garden.

We can well enter with the elder Jefferson and his confrères into the enthusiasm that thrilled them when they saw that fair land, at the foot of the mountains, and consisting of one sweetly rolling hill after another covered with magnificent timber, watered by numerous streams supplying power for their mills, bathed in tonic air as free of infection as any on earth. It was also quickly learned that on the slopes frosts seldom touched early in the spring or late in the autumn. It was a perfect country for agriculture and for pastoral life.

The influence of Jefferson is found here everywhere, fostering the erection of numerous edifices which are placed, every one, so as to take the largest advantage of site. They seem to fit and adorn the landscape more perfectly than elsewhere.

In the design of the central University building the guiding genius of Jefferson created what has stood unrivalled since his time as the most attractive edifice of any institution of learning. He got a double front, each very different from the other, all stepping down and leading away from the lovely central dome. The forecourt, honored by a bronze statue of him, is a gem of design. The other front, with its low rows of imposing pillared dormitories, is also like nothing else we have except as copied from this.

Jefferson doubtless suffered like all versatile geniuses from a diffusion of effort. But he could not of course keep close enough to his home affairs during many years' absence at the national capital. His financial interests were too broad to protect, in full; his ambition and generosity required a greater fortune. But we are glad that he never failed in public calls upon him. The improvident and the unfortunate lived upon him; he suffered the penalties of fame. But at least he was allowed the joy of dwelling in his beautiful home until the last. It is, of course, architecturally far finer than Mount Vernon, and though removed many miles farther from populous centers it is visited more than any other place in the South except Mount Vernon.

We observe that visitors to Charlottesville return once and again. The distinguished beauty of the homes about it, set in exquisite landscapes and enjoying a climate pleasing for so many months in the year, are altogether irresistible to visitors from North or South, East or West.

It is difficult to avoid superlatives at Charlottesville. Of course the captious will find imperfections and even the average traveler may think advertising features somewhat overdone, and the placing of sale furniture on the floors of Monticello a matter of questionable taste. But at any rate most things are as they should be in this improving world, around and about Charlottesville. In whatever direction one journeys there is so much good that the allowance of time is never sufficient.

For one thing perhaps nowhere else in America, in a region of so small a compass, have more men lived deserving well of their country. For the Tidewater section is larger. A veritable nest for hatching out presidents was this highland Virginian nook. And there were many more here capable of filling our highest office with honor. While we may be grateful for so many first class specimens of our race, we cannot but feel that scattering them would have been an advantage.

The stimulus of neighborhood example is an offsetting benefit where notably able men are dwelling near one another. Possibly a genius, living far from others like him, would have his light quenched in the general dimness around.

We should be thankful that we had a Jefferson. His life was not swallowed by holding office. He showed America, more than any man before him, or after him, how large an asset beauty is. There has been a great opportunity for our public men, not only to save the country, but to make it attractive afterwards, and it must be admitted that very few of them have lived up to their opportunity. When we consider the mean or sordid or tasteless environment with which the politicians and even statesmen have surrounded themselves we wish for more Jeffersons. Just as a jewel in the

AN OLD COUNTRY ROAD

ON THE ROANOKE, NEAR ROANOKE

dirt distresses our sense of fitness, so does the discovery that men in the public eye so seldom provide an example of fine taste in their homes, and in their avocations. Jefferson was always rounding a thought or a dome. He was producing a consistent fabric of state at the same time that he sought to surround society by those decencies and graces which make a state worth while. One sided men of course will be numerous enough, and in the scheme of things they may have their uses. But when Jefferson got liberty he used it in a liberal way. Life, liberty, and the pursuit of indolence is the manner in which an immortal phrase is wrenched aside. Jefferson found his happiness in doing beautiful work for himself and his neighbors. Those neighbors were of course all who were reached by his ideas. How many captains of industry have been captains of nothing else? Who is the foe of great architects? The great men who employ them but garble their work and throttle the aspirations which they wish to embody. Whoever builds a good wall or expresses perfectly a good thought makes all successive ages his debtors. It is time for all strong men not merely a few, to consider what they are to leave behind them, besides dollars. An amazingly large number of Americans have proved by their gifts that education appeals to them powerfully. Relatively few however have encouraged those intellectual pursuits which crown authorship, enrich the dwellings of the millions, and help the home by making it a lovely setting for life.

The Gothic age aimed at ecclesiastical exaltation through its edifices. We have been waiting for a passion to break out aimed at housing all the people with dignity, embellished by beauty, conserved by solidity. The ages have had their various passions. If this passion ever rises it will allow the sun to look down on a forward movement that should easily surpass in two generations all similar progress in human history.

The multitudes are crying for luxuries, but they are not yet craving for necessities. Human frills not human dignity interest them mostly. If they would direct half of their present expenditure for noise and movement toward repose and permanence and beauty the wealth of America could soon create a new world. Limiting thought to Virginia the whole state could be what the environs of Charlottesville are. Such a future is coming. How many souls will be battered, how many ages will pass before such a consummation we do not know. But at any rate we can refuse to put our hand to any but good work, and refuse to kill time.

OAK SPANDREL, KENMORE   TUCKAHOE FIREPLACE

KENMORE

PALM SPANDREL

THE QUARTERS

A BLOOMING CHURCHYARD

GRAPE SPANDREL

OLD DUTCH DOOR

THE LOCUST CURVE

MISTLETOE SPANDREL CEILING

GOV. SPOTSWOOD'S PEW

A WILLIAMSBURG RETREAT

WARREN HOUSE

ON PAGE ninety-four, we have placed a drawing for the tentative restoration of the Warren House, which lies in Surrey County at no very great distance from Bacon's Castle. This is in that soft open country with oaks here and there south of the James, which makes a little kingdom of itself. This house is said to have been built in 1654. It is of brick, and on a gentle slope so that in the rear there is a good basement. At the present time the dwelling is not in a very bad condition so far as its principal lines are concerned. But the steps, front and back, the front door, and doorhead, and the old sash and shutters are all lacking. We have placed a very simple doorhead in position. It resembles that of the side door of the hall at Tuckahoe. At this period we know that the diamond pane, leaded glass, was that generally in use, and we know that a house as early as this would have had solid shutters. My talented secretary, Mr. Ernest John Donnelly, has made this drawing as well as all other sketches in the volume. It is done not with any pretension, but on a basis of a very wide experience with old houses. If the date given this house is correct it is perhaps not surpassed in age by any dwelling except the Thoroughgood House in Norfolk County, near Lynhaven. It must be admitted that that house looks much older than this. It is perhaps a quarter of a mile from the highway, and the estate was previously owned by the son of Pocahontas. If it was built by John Rolfe, his father, it has a greatly added interest, and in that case it is altogether the most romantic house in Virginia. It will be remembered that Pocahontas was taken to England. It is a mystery that descendants of Pocahontas whose blood flows through several notable Virginia families, did not secure and restore this house. It is said now to be in the hands of a wealthy well wisher of Virginia, but not one of the family. A dwelling like this was of course intended for a small manor. It was for the use of the family only, all the servants sleeping in outside quarters. It is a charming little place, where love in a cottage might prove a romantic reality.

NAMES

THE classical tale of the negro mother who named her son after half of the presidents, so that his initials (as he would make them) formed a crazy picket fence across a page, reveals a woman who was a philosopher.

Anything as easily captured as a name ought to be the spoil of any woman's spear, and might as well be a good name as a poor one. But names seem to be left till the last thing or to be the sport of accident or incident. One day we noticed, so great was our interest in the scenery, that the gasoline had run too low. One of us said, we shall have a scrabble to reach the next station. As we rounded the next hill, and saw a pump ahead, what do you suppose was the name of that neighborhood, on a fine painted sign? Believe it or not, it was Scrabble. The names of a region embed its history. One thinks of the Puritan nomenclature as confined to a narrow range. By no means. In Virginia the surname Mourning appears, and *Lancaster* mentions him as an undertaker. But soft, that meant contractor! We have in John Smyth's narration and in the parish records, all the names for a new Pilgrim's or Rogue's progress, from Resolution and Condolence to Diana and Ananias. If the name was in the Bible it was regarded as thoroughly fumigated by the connection, though it may have been borne by the worst villain unhung.

One of the Virginia instances of adulation galore, was that of naming two contiguous counties, the one Patrick, the other Henry!

In the older parts of the state there ought to be no furniture except the Dutch, for King William, King and Queen, and the names and titles of the royal children or relations cover the country, and at Williamsburg we crown all in the Duke of Gloucester street! Most of the English counties are repeated here, with a generous quota left over, in the west, for the Revolutionary heroes.

When we add the river names, very generally Indian, the names from the old homes of the continental settlers, like Strasburg and Mecklenburg, we have a joyous medley, with enough to satisfy all. But the poetic mind also asserted itself, so that Afton (we went thirty miles to see it owing to the name), Gladys, Nellysford, Amelia and such appellations abound. But we wonder what disgusted railroad man named a station Bumpass? or who chose Ammon? or Hurt? or Skippers? or who upset the tin peddler's cart into Hardware River? But also the old name of the river was not Rapidan but Rapid Anne! What a libel on a staid queen!

The names of the plantations were often happily chosen. Some were given by gallant husbands, after the maiden names of their wives. Does this hint that they brought fat dowries? Others like Hopewell were based on anticipations of good fortune in a new country. Some names are so good that estates could almost subsist on them.

The mariner arriving from a tempestuous voyage would in thankful

AN ALLEGHANY FARM

UNDER THE MOUNTAINS, TAZEWELL

THE INTAKE, NORTHERN NECK

BOX DRIVE, MT. BERNARD

IN THE TOE OF VIRGINIA

EASTER DOGWOOD, PITTSYLVANIA

mood easily dub a propitious landfall Old Point or New Point Comfort. And those names flavor the thought of many generations. Of course the carelessness or poverty of the human mind too often appeared in the repetition of an old name without end, until it meant nothing distinctive. There ought to be one more commission—one on names, to see to it that dignity, euphony, and originality if possible be considered in fixing a name which, being borne for a great while, may as well be good as bad.

An acquaintance is so apt in the matter that he is often appealed to. A good many new abodes in a state need names every year. Why repeat Buckingham or Belmont till everybody sighs and wishes a place had been named scat?

As an instance of the supremacy in men's minds of the occupation of grazing, notice Cowpasture River, Calfpasture River, Bull Run, and Pig River. As the origin of a famous grape there is Catawba, River and town.

A little attention to names, even to the naming of children, would add a great deal to the dignity and decoration of life. In Catholic countries all intellectual effort is spared in this respect by naming a child for its saint's day.

The Siamese Accomac House (page 181) is an excellent suggestion for simple cottage architecture, which the author does not happen to have seen outside of Accomac County where he noticed in a single day, a dozen such houses, as alike as two peas. The connecting link is often in the same roof pitch as the ends, a simplification much desired, and an assistance in giving greater dignity to the house which should not look too much like two cottages tied fortuitously together. The porch may be only in the connection, or may extend along the entire front, or as here may be in front of the connection and extend along one end section. The author was so much attracted by this type that he would like to copy it in brick with chimneys at the outside ends, as in some instances it occurs. There is room for just the right amount of vine decoration.

A Fronded Cone (page 182) seen in the southwest is not alone in the charm of its form. Sometimes a half dozen such evenly tapering peaks are in sight at once. They never appear as barren rocks but always as softly wooded, with fields of grass or grain running up irregularly on their slopes, sometimes to the very summits. They form a feature so pleasing as to rival anything else seen in Virginia. They are the more dear, as they cluster below the mountains, as a rule, and seem like overtures of affection to beg one to love and stay near them. The view is so general that a little cottage in the village scarcely appears. But in blossom time, and fruit time what a delightful background for life!

A Virginia Forest Drive (page 185) is found near Scottsville on the James and is the country road approach to a number of retired estates like Tallwood, Enniscorthy, and so forth. It is the laurel that spreads itself on the right for our delectation, and the shapeless moving shadows are for any soul who loves them. Who loves them not?

THE SHENANDOAH

A MOUTH filling word, whose rolling syllables incarnate grandeur and romance! So full has been the vocabulary describing the Shenandoah that whatever one says of it he will say less than has been said. It is so fine that it is a pity to try to compare it with scenery wholly different. It has nothing Alpine in its composition. It is nearer and warmer.

While limited properly to that valley drained by the river of the same name there is in effect on the traveler one valley, from its beginning at Harper's Ferry and the Potomac almost to the extreme southwest of the state, and embracing those other basins which send their waters south and west.

The love of classification arises from mental indolence. Every object in nature is individual. The joy of life is, properly, the observance of distinctions. The old geographers, as in Jefferson's Virginia, loved to mark their mountain ranges as if they were composed of identical units following one another in single file without a deviation.

But uniformity is abhorrent to nature, so that we must admire every mountain, every stream, every human face for itself and discover its peculiar lines, its character marks.

The Blue Ridge, in general the southeastern barrier of the Shenandoah, and the Appalachians, more or less fencing the valley on the northwest, are names of tumbled masses and by no means serried ranks. They advance or retreat at their own sweet will; they are lofty or moderate in elevation, they afford bays of lowlands or jut out in promontories on the plains, they approach their opposite companions till there is scarce room for the river to squeeze between, or they lie so far apart that we forget we are in a valley at all. And besides all that they open in such manner as to admit subordinate

A SHENANDOAH GATE

WAKEFIELD MONUMENT

ON THE BLUE RIDGE

THE LANDING

streams, and grant many a delightful passage into the outside world. To define the Shenandoah is an impossible and an unnecessary task. It is better merely to admire it, and to select here and there a dimple or a contour that catches our fancy.

For four hundred miles the esthete may follow the windings of this valley so full of beautiful surprises, but never tame. He never knows when he passes out of it and is in fact in some other valley, unless he notices that the direction of the streams has changed.

I imagine the people and the valleys to the southwest do not wholly relish being included in the Shenandoah, when they are not of it. No matter, like Moses' rod, it seems to swallow up its subordinate relatives, and its name goes far. It is easier for the languid mind to group the entire western part of Virginia as the Valley, spelled always with a capital by custom, from respect and to save time.

For one, though my own people were participants, I would like to think less about those marchings, and countermarchings, when armed men picked their painful and violent way up and down between these rebuking hills, astonished at their violators. Two generations are, or ought to be, enough to allow us to forget the differences while admiring the stubborn heroisms of our fathers.

The fertility of the whole region has covered the wounds with bowing, yellow grain, or bearded over the scars by feathery forests, and luxuriant creepers. The entire year's season offers its succession of panoramic beauty. The ill named Judas tree sprinkles the roadside with its inimitable tint, following the scattering white of the shad bush. The wild and tame cherry, the pink and white surge of apple blossoms, the grace of the two locusts, yellow or white, the procession of the blackberry blooms, like white lace edging the garments of the later spring, the exuberance of the rose, all following fast each on each, are the shifting curtain in this theatre of beauty. The dogwood is, however, even more extensive and more beautiful than any of the other natural decorations.

As each of these aspects of delight unfold one says "I did not believe there were so many Judas trees in the world"; or "here are apples to refresh a nation"; or "the entire country is covered with locust," that hardiest, daintiest among shade trees.

The traveler should not expect to be often skirting nor always even in sight of the rivers. Their courses are too devious and hidden to be much in evidence.

VIRGINIA BEAUTIFUL

As in a day's effort to follow the Thames we scarce ever reached it, and as in going down the James we came only at long intervals to its banks, so here. The path of the stream is not the path of men, unless they love it so well as to guide a canoe through its secret windings. Nor is there a sameness in the men who dwell here. English, Irish, Scotch, German, and doubtless others were among the early settlers, usurping the surprised and resentful Indian, who must follow his sad western trail first into Kentucky and at length to the utmost bounds to make room for this plowing, building, dominating European. At length all these human and vegetable elements have learned to live together. Probably no other section of America can exhibit such a succession of substantial farm houses as rise along the main highway. By the broad foresight of the state the toll on the pike has been abolished. Unrestricted, the valley is ready to share its good things with all who list to explore it. But as ever, and wisely, the best in nature is not too obvious. Often only to the reverent eye are the finest treasures, natural or divine, unveiled. The rushing tourist, thinking only of an antique or a watering place, may pass unheeded charms fit to thrill the lover of the beautiful with day enduring ecstasies.

The very indefiniteness of the skyline tops our view with nature's age-long lure of mystery, which she knows so well how to use. Beginning with the most obvious roadside cottage and Virginia rail fence, she carries our eyes along to scan the farther farms, the high pastoral slopes, the lofty dignity of the remoter heights, until at length she leads us to those evanescent masses, are they peaks or are they clouds or are they the outskirts of the mystic seas and shores of an unknowable realm where beauty is always in the ascendant and the spirits of supermen clothe themselves in the garments of the sunset? The glory and the charm of life consist in this: that it is always a border land to a richer reality, a city of the skies, a hem of the universe, just broad enough for us to take hold of, and unfolding a splendor, a power in every atom of the world, a harmony reaching between what we know and what we know is far beyond our knowing.

It is not for naught that the more southern mountains are called the Great Smokies. They help man to claim his heritage of a creature of imagination as well as a tiller of the ground. Dreams are a means of lifting lighter and lacier architecture in the dome of thought and of catching our lassos to a sunset. Mountain regions ought to be denizened by poets, and doubtless there are plenty of them here, possibly mute, but not altogether inglorious.

Jefferson and his confrères felt the advantage of fixing their abodes on rising ground, where the humdrum can be more easily yoked with the imaginative; the one being lifted, the other being chastened by the connection, so that while men's feet were on the ground their heads might be in the clouds.

The Shenandoah! If it did not whisper prophecy as well as record history it would not be a tithe as fascinating. And consider what a change has come over it in a generation. From a closed valley it has become a Mecca for America. The national forests, present and prospective, that fringe it, the developing wealth of its soil, its opening on the mineral treasures of the southwest of the state, its vestibule to the great resorts of the Hot Springs, the Warm and Sulphur Springs, its caverns, opening to an underworld of beauty and imagination, are a present reality and they afford a solid foundation for growth into a far broader development. It contains one county bearing the name Shenandoah. Its suggestions, however, of breadth, extent and development cover many other aspects of life dear to the Virginian who has always been poetic.

West of the Blue Ridge something like a third of the State of Virginia is located. If we consider that part of the state between the Blue Ridge and Tidewater Virginia, a region consisting of rolling plains, we get in the two sections a good deal more than half of the state. Historically, however, Tidewater Virginia has been dominant, and with the growth of the Norfolk area and the Richmond area no doubt the dominance of the older Virginia will continue for a good many years. In the long future prospect one would say that at length the western part of the state may prove the more important. That is not especially pertinent. We only desire to see every county of Virginia reach its high possible goal as the home of a race grown rich in cultural advantages and that inevitable strength and beauty which ever results when a people and a land react upon one another until one feels that the virtue of each has passed into the other, and one admires the country on account of its people and what they have added to it, and its people on account of what they have attained to by the cleverest use of their natural advantages.

Beginning at Winchester with its blossom festival and following the mountain region to its going out at Cumberland Gap into Tennessee and Kentucky, one sees that the northeastern end of this reach has so far received the greater share of national attention.

It was a fine conception, largely we suppose, due to the former Governor Byrd, to celebrate by a great festival the apple bloom. The writer has for many years emphasized the preëminence of eastern America as a country of unequaled beauty in apple blossom time, so much so indeed that in a dozen states for a third of a century he has depicted and sent out in color the choicer scenes of orchard beauty. It is, therefore, with keen joy and appreciation that he sees the Virginians, led by the Byrds, taking the first step in formal recognition of this most superb efflorescence of our American world, the apple tree. It is not to the credit of the northern states, supposedly rich in artistic appreciation, that they have left to Virginia this first general and forward recognition of blossom time. But we rejoice in the fact that the Byrds, foremost so often, are also foremost here. Their success in this particular is outstanding, so much so that Washingtonians seem to consider that apples grow beautifully nowhere except about Winchester. This concentration of public attention on the most attractive aspect of American life was a happy stroke of genius, no less so that it made famous the apples following the blossoms.

That we live in a world of contest was demonstrated this spring as the author was attempting a new sweep through the valley to record the beauties of the season. A blighting frost in one night browned the blossoms on millions of trees till not only the orchard owners, but sympathetic visitors could scarcely restrain their tears. The mystery whereby "one shall be taken and another left" appeared in many orchards wherein some trees retained the glory of their bloom side by side with trees that were smitten.

Up the valley (which one always thinks of as down, like "down South") Woodstock is the acme of the purely rural Shenandoah. The tourist loses what is no doubt the best joy of a journey unless he makes his way up many of the narrower roads to the little villages that cluster under the hills.

The passages out of the Shenandoah are often more beautiful than the valley itself. One would say that about Millwood in Clarke County is one of the fairest districts before we reach the mountains. Riverton and Front Royal, twin towns, are at a point where the river, the park and the valley meet and where the north and south fork converge. Then there is the passage from New Market to Luray. From Harrisonburg we may go west into West Virginia over the ridge, and east to Elkton and Gordonsville. At Staunton also one finds delightful cross journeys either way, to Churchville and Buffalo Gap, or to Waynesboro and Charlottesville. We really pass over the northern and southern water shed between Staunton and Lexington. The beauty of the southwest district, however, is superior to that of the Shenandoah Valley proper.

ORCHARD ZIG ZAGS NEAR STAUNTON

THE MONTPELIER POOL

HOME OF THE WARNERS, WASHINGTON'S GRANDPARENTS

AN UPPER BRANDON DRIVE

A NORFOLK STREET

WESTOVER SHORE

A GABLE OF ROSES, SHADWELL

A SOUTHERN GABLE, NEAR WINCHESTER

A LAUREL POOL

LYNCHBURG MEMORIALS BULL RUN BRIDGE

A PITTSYLVANIA CAMP

HOME FROM SCHOOL   IN THE OLD DOMINION

SHENANDOAH NATURAL PARK

LAUREL FOREST   A GARDEN BORDER, MT. AIRY

WE GROW OLD

NOTES ON THE PICTURES

THE Gilbert Place (page 150) near Danville, we have not noticed as appearing in any previous work on Virginia, but owing to the oddity and to some degree the merit of its architecture it is worthy of record. It will be seen that the central portion is two stories high, the roof line presenting its gable to the front which is in the form of a portico with a subordinate porch beneath. So far we follow conventional lines. Now at either side is a one story wing, the roof lines presenting gables and being brought forward nearly to the front of the great pillars. The effect is most unusual and, set back by a good approach through fine trees, is rather impressive.

Three Gables (page 164) represents one end of Willow Lawn, Winchester, the other and totally different end being shown as a Southern Gable (page 114).

The former picture, the service end of the house, shows the two outside chimneys in the main end gable, with vines, and a one story and dormer ell with a porch suggesting Dutch types. The opposite end shows a two story ell with a two story recessed porch possessing merits for southern life. The front, not shown, as somewhat too obscured by foliage for a good pictorial presentation, exhibits an extended edifice of much variety and attraction.

Powell's River Banks (page 189) is one of numerous beautiful stretches of the leisurely stream, which though it be among the mountains, seems to find a gentle course to the outer world. The finest and most numerous river scenes are in the uplands of Virginia. There it is often necessary for the road to take advantage of the way the stream has made between the crests. A highway is too independent when it may reach out across a plain with never a "by your leave" to hill or rock.

Governor Spotswood's Pew

There is, or was, a deeper reason for stateliness and ceremony than the gratification of the participants. England is a very democratic country, but the state with which the judge and sheriff parade through the streets or take their places in court, stands for the majesty of the law; it represents the sovereign power; and while the outward show tends in the minds of many to have its effect, the deeper reason behind it all is the dignity and grandeur of the state as standing for order and righteousness. The judge in boots, lifted as high as his head, and seated in a shabby room, gives an impression that the state itself lacks dignity.

Governor Spotswood's pew (page 98) with its magnificent crimson canopy and its chair of great elaboration and richness, was not so much for the governor himself as that which he represented. This chair, by the way, is a remarkable example of its period, sometime before the Revolution. The other chair is the precious possession of a masonic society and is left here, it is said, for reasons of safety. Above the chairs are seen the gilded arms of England. Near by, to carry out, in modern days, the old tradition, there is a Bible presented by Edward VII, and a brass lectern presented by President Roosevelt. Such things are not without their use. The revolt of the Puritan age against such pomp arose out of the fear that the people would mistake the trappings for the things which they represented. The danger was a very real one, and is no less to be guarded against today. The untrained mind, which now and always has been in the vast majority, confounds the outward show with a solid reality which lies behind it. Of course simplicity with dignity is the ideal condition. But because it is an ideal, it is not attained by the many.

The officials of the church have always enjoyed working with the officials of the state, each supporting the others, by their laws or liturgies, and after awhile insensibly oppressing the average mind. The golden mean is the rarest condition to be met with. Church and state always arrogate too much or claim too little authority. License and bigotry are easy extremes. The conservative is ever in danger of congealing; the radical is ever in danger of exploding.

THE YORKTOWN CUSTOM HOUSE

IT IS much to the credit of the patriotic people of Virginia, that through many obstacles they have persisted and secured so many restorations. Mrs. Chenowith of Yorktown has enthusiastically championed this effort with loyal helpers whom the writer has the misfortune of not knowing.

The custom house is a perfect little specimen of a very early colonial edifice, in the favorite Flemish bond. Very recent discoveries even now are revealing other contiguous buildings which it is thought may have been brick sheds or store houses in connection with the custom house. It is the

earliest building now standing devoted to revenue collecting in our country, and it is even said that at one time it was the port of entry for New York! Yet it dates from 1715 when New York had a history of about a hundred years behind it. One supposes the meaning may be that the officer here was given charge over a coast-wide area.

Yorktown was once the center of a good number of rich dwellings nearly all of which met their fate in the bombardment directed at Cornwallis, from land and water. Indeed it was the best peppered town in the colonies, for let no one suppose that Cornwallis surrendered except under dire necessity; the lines were so completely established that the annihilation of the town and his army was certain.

The great national monument, somewhat ornate, is recent. The Digges House, the Nelson House (York Hall) and its dependencies, the church and the Moore House, the place of surrender, constitute the principal relics of the place. Yet the York River is one of the few sheltered harbors, unused, capable of receiving modern ships.

In time of war as in the last great war, York River was found very convenient as a safe anchorage. It seems to be a case of a wonderful harbor not ordinarily needed.

THE CITY DWELLINGS

THERE really were no cities in Virginia in the old time. Williamsburg, the seat of government and the focus of society, was a small village. There was no need and no desire for cities. Manufacturing was carried on to a considerable degree by trained servants on the plantations. Spinning, weaving, the making of all the servants' garments, shoe making, common harness making, wagon work, blacksmithing, malting and flour grinding was done in every great establishment. The finer manufactures being derived from England, and the middle class being small, there was little demand for shops or factories. As on Russian estates before the revolution every plantation was sufficient unto itself, except for the luxuries demanded by the owner's family. For this reason the town house could be exactly like the country house, or if used only in the social season, could be built on a smaller scale. That is how land values in the towns permitted a generous width of lot and as in Williamsburg, the dwellings showed their long fronts to the streets. Kenmore in Fredericksburg occupied a block of land! The county

PENNINGTON GAP   THE OAK AT THE BEND

A VALLEY ORCHARD

ROSEHILL GARDEN   THE ROANOKE

THE MOUNTAIN COTTAGE NEST

seats were so generally composed of dominant courthouses and little else, that the curious condition resulted of naming a shire town for the courthouse.

The city house in the usual understanding of that term did not appear to any extent until well into the nineteenth century, as in Richmond. It is therefore almost wholly beyond the scope of this work which naturally could not occupy itself with modern dwellings however beautiful, and beautiful they are in Richmond, Norfolk, Roanoke, Lynchburg and many other growing cities.

I think we may attribute the great beauty and excellent taste of the Richmond dwellings of this generation to the examples, so numerous and so near at hand, of fine eighteenth century work. One has inevitably impressed upon him, that the Virginian carries on the gracious traditions of the past and is seeking to conserve the best of the eighteenth for the twentieth century. That is how civilization grows, by cumulative effect, for no one generation can plan or execute all the desirable achievements.

Driving about Richmond one is amazed at the innumerable beautiful houses, superior in number and quality, perhaps, to those found in any other American city of its population. And this is the more astonishing and gratifying, because only recently has wealth come to Richmond. It proves that its people know where and how to use their wealth.

One can only hope that this influence will spread to that area south and fanwise from Richmond, where in the country the thought of an attractive home seems not so much in evidence.

WARM SPRINGS IN VIRGINIA

FROM early times the virtues of warm or hot springs in Virginia have been recognized, but it is a curious fact, here, and in Europe, away back in the classical day, on the Continent and at Bath in England, the remedial aspects have been swallowed up in the social aspects. Fashion rules, and when fashion ceases for a time to dictate a particular resort, as Saratoga, the virtues of the heat or the minerals are entirely forgotten.

Meantime the seeker after beauty is benefited in this, that persons of means establish beautiful estates about the springs and enhance whatever nature did for herself, and she has done more than enough to entrance us in Virginia.

VIRGINIA BEAUTIFUL

The new drive through the lower part of the Shenandoah National Forest and Goshen Pass to the Springs is almost a continual joy. Jackson's River a tributary of the James makes its way through all the ridges of the Alleghanies, and pierces also the Blue Ridge, on its way past Natural Bridge to the James. It perhaps forms more scenes of beauty than any other stream in the East, not even excepting the Hudson. The sources of the Jackson-James in Highland County are so remote that the river is a very long one. The fact that it has made its way through a succession of many mountain barriers proves the irregularity and the moderate elevations of all these crests.

Coming out of Covington one passes the exquisitely lovely Falling Spring, which, before and at its leap is perhaps the most attractive body of water in Virginia, though others to be mentioned have their special charms. The cultivated slopes about the Springs hold one's eye, and lingeringly we scan these perfect cones, rank on rank, behind one another, those more remote showing their heads peeping forth like a class of college girls pictured at graduation.

Two or three miles from Covington on the road to the Hot Springs, as one looks back, the finest mass of tumbled mountains appears. It seemed to us the supreme scene of its kind in Virginia, or perhaps anywhere. It is best viewed in the forenoon. Here one looks down into the successive hollows and across the cones almost as a gardener looks down at the hills of his planting. It is worth going a thousand miles to see. Mile for mile, where can the match of this road be found?

The drive to Sulphur Springs is also quite worth while. All this part of Virginia is even finer than the Valley itself, since one is directly in contact with the mountains.

The spirit of the mountaineer, always the spirit of liberty, steals on us without our knowledge. We easily understand how a mountain country has never long suffered tyranny without revolt and how Switzerland has been a republic for six hundred years.

In a nook in the mountains the physical enclosure, forming a little world in itself, a domain easy of defence, tends to foster an intense patriotism such as dwellers on level lands never knew. When were patriots to the fore in Mesopotamia or Egypt? But the emphasis on individuals in a broken country is constant. It is every man for himself to carve out his destiny and that of his mountain state within his own horizon, watched over by the sentinel peaks with whose dependable and glorious outlines he has been

A NATURAL DAM

OGLE CREEK, SULPHUR SPRINGS

THE MILL CANAL

LEBANON VALLEY

familiar from babyhood. Mountain men are not to be conquered, nor if conquered will they remain static. It is said that in some Appalachian counties every able bodied man, and that number included some past age, has volunteered in case of war. The cliffs are suggested in the strong faces of these mountain dwellers. Even in peace they must fight to maintain their hold on the narrow valleys.

The true blue of the sparkling streams is seen in their eyes. They live without the luxuries of the board but they inherit and maintain the larger luxury of freedom. It is theirs to behold every morning the play of wisps of vapor about the summits, serried with evergreens. It is theirs to see the breaks of blue opening in rolling masses of summer cloud and closing again after giving one glance at the virgin breasts of the hills. It is theirs to answer with their own eye flashes the levin bolt when the storms struggle about their peaks. It is theirs to echo the calls of the storm, and to joy in the white torrents that pour down the gorges of their private world. Can there be any question that such a land is a breeder of brave, reticent men, with reserve power, and steady faith? And if the fields are narrow and must be cultivated betwixt crag and stream, what better crop can a country produce than such men? They have been the strength of Scotland and America in time past, and it will be a sad day for us when we cease to see the advantage of the mountain home.

LEXINGTON AND THE NATURAL BRIDGE

THEY are separated but little. At both and at almost every important tourist point in Virginia are good hotels. One never ceases to be surprised that at Winchester, Harrisonburg, Staunton, and the various springs, at Roanoke, and away south at Wytheville, Bristol and even Appalachia are modern inns, fit for the fastidious. That towns of less than ten thousand persons should be so provided causes a pleased surprise. Lexington is attractive in itself, and for its surroundings. There is always a lure about a small town which is a seat of learning. In this case the attraction is more than doubled by the association of Lee with the university which has added his name to that of Washington. There he is buried, and to his tomb a large and reverent multitude pay their pilgrimages.

A cottage in the hills here offers to one retiring from business a delightful fellowship with the faculty, who welcome outside associations as an agreeable diversion.

Seated in view of House Mountain, in short reach of the various springs, faced by a main range on either hand, close to the incomparable Natural Bridge and its National Forest, within moderate distance of teeming Lynchburg over one of the world's most beautiful drives, contiguous to rich farms and orchards, Lexington is certainly such a center in Virginia as is comparable with Charlottesville alone.

Jefferson, with his fine appreciative mind, both for natural scenery and architecture, secured possession of the Natural Bridge, and only deeded it away with the thought that it would be preserved for posterity. It is one of the few objects in nature that is not too extravagantly praised. The traveler little suspects that his main road takes him directly over this bridge. Grandeur, beauty, romance are all assembled here.

Compared with the Zion National Park in Utah, the Natural Bridge of course is not so impressive for mass. Those who wrote about it many years ago, did so before the Utah wonders were known. The baldness, however, of the Western scenery detracts more from its admirable qualities than the larger dimensions add. Furthermore, consider the delight of living in a fine climate, in a college town, and within a few minutes drive not only of the Natural Bridge, but of caverns, mountains, meadows and charming farm lands!

NOTES ON PICTURES

A Gable of Roses, Shadwell (page 114). Shadwell was the first Jefferson place when Peter, the father of Thomas, migrated to the Piedmont from Tidewater. Though the original dwelling has disappeared the later one is not new, and it is a pleasure to find it in the hands of gentle people, appreciative of the past, and honoring the ancestors by reproducing their best virtues. The roses about the guest house are the most luxuriant that we saw in Virginia.

A Pittsylvania Camp (page 116). Whether some settler erected this log house as a permanent home, or whether it was placed here at the edge of the woods as a refuge, we do not know. We feel, however, more and more that the rush and swirl and racket of our day, is likely to take away creative power such as arises from reflection and an undisturbed working out of some subject worth while. The tides of history have turned and they may turn again to send people away from the centers. In fact the modern trend of

THE HOUSE BY THE SIDE OF THE ROAD

OPEN GATES TO WINCHESTER

THE FLOUNCES OF DOROTHY PERKINS

BY THE GATE

A BLUE RIDGE ORCHARD

MORVEN DRIVE

THE WAY OF THE EARTH

ACROSS THE UPLANDS

young and old towards summer camps at least provides an aggreable change, however much it may stimulate intellectual effort.

The Way of the Earth (page 134), is another of those abandoned log houses that are awaiting the coming of a summer guest, whose interest will be in rendering such a place habitable. The location is not far east of Danville. One can see how much joy would be derived from reëstablishing living conditions in and about such a dear old cabin to afford a refuge for the summer season at least.

Sabine Hall in Richmond County (page 148) has often been well described, and we pause here merely to mention its salient features. It is another of the numerous Carter places. We show the garden front which during the week of visitation is opened. The house has an attractive interior, the stair opening from the side of the great hall, a frequent Southern fashion, rather than in it. In its earliest features the place dates from about 1730, but of course must have been changed somewhat. It contains notable portraits.

QUARTERS NEAR LYNCHBURG

IN THE investigation of the old South the house servants' quarters frequently appeal to one as picturesque. They were often of logs, or covered with vines. It seemed impossible in the eighteenth ecntury to build otherwise than in good taste and with some motive or other that fixes our attention and wins our approval. Here the two storied quarters have exterior stairs under canopies. As the stair was repeated at the other end a balanced structure resulted, attractive in design. The exterior stair avoided direct communication between the floors and saved the complete space for use on both floors.

Sometimes all these dependent buildings, with ice house, coach house, kitchen and school were of brick, as at Stratford. Sometimes they were mostly of wood as at Tuckahoe. But always they followed a well laid out plan, so that the entire group formed a pleasing assemblage, each separate edifice setting off another as a seemingly necessary part of the whole. The smokehouse was of wood.

Naturally these accessories of the old plantation are rapidly disappearing, since the servants now live, as a rule, at a greater distance. It is good therefore to preserve as examples the types that remain.

ZIG ZAG SHADOWS

IT IS noticeable that the zig zag fence which has acquired the name Virginia rail is being brought to the fore, as a decorative feature, and is at times extended to the very gates of an estate. Probably it is the most picturesque fence known, except a boulder stone wall. The rail fence acquired its popularity because it could be shifted with ease and dispatch whenever needed, even more rapidly than the English hurdle fence. But when it is allowed to gather decorative vines at its angles it becomes an object of real attraction. When the late shadows fall athwart (page 231) on a ribbon lane, the climax of quaint decoration results.

Stones, the handicap of farming in so many regions, are wholly absent from the greater part of Virginia, but occasionally in the Valley they were built into fences which became beautiful with the columbine or the blackberry, which latter follows fair blossom with dark fruit, each a joy.

One may say that after the trees the rail fences are the most attractive feature of Virginia. Then follow the billowing fields of bright golden grain.

Of course among the woodlands, the dogwood, I believe the state flower, is by its abundance and its clear white against green, a chief delight.

WHERE TO FIND BEAUTY

IT TAKES a deal of investigating to learn that most of the fine scenery of Virginia is in a quarter of her counties, and that most of her fine old dwellings are in a tenth of her counties. Out of a hundred counties the entire rank, usually double, of thirty counties, that march northeast on the mountain side, contain most of the scenery. The counties of James City, York, Gloucester, Accomac, Charles City, Stafford, Fairfax, Albemarle, Clarke and Frederick, less than a tenth of the area of the state, contain perhaps nine-tenths of the fine early dwellings, Henrico, where Richmond is situated, is notable historically, and for the early nineteenth century type, and is therefore omitted from the first ten, it being not so old. Thus *Lancaster* in his work omits entirely, from illustrating, about forty counties, and of various others he shows one example.

The person therefore who has a month to tour Virginia will go from Richmond along the James to York, cross the ferry, take in the neck between the York and the Rappahannock to Tappahannock. Cross the bridge and get Richmond (County) and Westmoreland, and go on to Fredericksburg and thence through Fairfax to Winchester and so on southwest as far as time permits, returning by the more northwestern, nearly parallel, route through Lebanon, Bluefields, Covington, the various springs, Staunton, (first point of touching down route). Thence Charlottesville, Orange, and Warrenton for Washington direct, or Richmond from Charlottesville. Whoever makes this journey, omitting nothing within very short runs of the main track, will have seen some hundred notably fine houses and the best of Virginia landscapes.

This schedule allows a month. Two months are needed to do it fairly. Two journeys, one for the Tidewater, one for the remainder of the state, would be better. Of course the things seen will be cursorily viewed. A number of the finest places are not open to the public, except by invitation or correspondence.

Garden week in Virginia is a brief time, but in that week, as one pays a fee for patriotic restorations, one feels less embarrassment in entering private grounds.

Mount Vernon (except on Sunday), Fredericksburg, the Williamsburg-Jamestown places are as much on view at one time as another, and Charlottesville is always open.

As to the season there seems only one perfect season, the world over, the spring. The apple blossom time is too early for most of the other vegetation, but a six weeks' period would span all good foliage. The next best time is the autumn, not before October, nor after for that matter. If this route may fairly be considered to include Norfolk or Newport News to gain their hotels, the traveler may have a modern hotel every night but one, and that night may be comfortable. There is only one ferry on this route, and that is good and on smooth water. Not every mile will win on the traveler, but there will be hard road nearly all the way, and good gravel for the small remainder. The older Virginia cement roads were not laid out wide enough, but that fault is being rapidly corrected.

Persons who prefer to make Richmond a headquarters for the northern and middle neck, need never change their hotel for the Tidewater section, after two or three days' excursions from Washington to the near points in Virginia. Many persons choose as centers Washington, Richmond, a city at the mouth of the James, Charlottesville, Winchester, Lexington, Wytheville. But of course the various springs are finely fitted to receive one, and on the main line Harrisonburg, Staunton, Natural Bridge, Roanoke, have their favorites, and even remote Appalachia is good. The writer was at all these points and many others, for the night, or longer.

Richmond is one of the best hotel cities of America, and probably supreme among cities of her size.

Omitting the triple center, Old Point Comfort, Hampton and Newport News, there is not a city between the whole reach from the Potomac to the James in Tidewater. I do not mean that there is no town corporation but the populations are village size, yet nearly all the land teems with good farms. That is the charm of the country, that it is country. When we reach villages sometimes we wish they were not there. The attractive village in the South, since it does not contain the homes of the old families, is infrequent.

There are fifteen counties, perhaps, in Virginia, without railroads, and ten of these are the contiguous northern and middle neck counties, of the Tidewater.

A PROTECTED BANK

CROSSING THE APPALACHIANS

VIRGINIA WINDINGS

A LITTLE MOUNTAIN VALLEY

This is a delightful anomaly in America, for these are among the very oldest counties in all our country. But let no stranger mistake this fact as an evidence of backwoods conditions. There are fine cultivation and dwellings almost everywhere, but the peculiarity is that the region is so intersected with tidal and navigable waters that the plantations are nearer a market than most sections well supplied with railroads. There are of course roads, mostly good, but from of old the waters, not closed by frost, not affected by freshet, not susceptible of being monopolized, and handy to the great markets of the world, have been the great and unique asset of these counties. Whatever modes of conveyance are devised in the future, water carriage here will always be the main reliance, at the same time that it is accompanied by a romance and charm not otherwise found. Williamsburg is rapidly becoming beautiful; but it is unique; always was and always will be. Jamestown is not a village, consisting of memorials only. Yorktown is redeemed, but it is a very tiny village.

Moving northerly we find Gloucester has some good features; Readsville is quite dapper. In the upper country Warrenton, Culpepper and Orange make in some degree, an appeal, yet the basal development of Virginia was not the village, but the plantation. The middle class was relatively small. The beauty is largely off the road. The churches were built apart to accommodate the people of several plantations. There were few to build or inhabit sedate streets of widely detached substantial eight room houses. We must look for those pleasing features which the nature of the country and the occupations and training of the planter tended to develop. The failure to do so accounts for the disappointment of some visitors from the north or middle west. They are looking for the same aspects of life that they find at home. They will look in vain. They will find the beauty of lower Virginia in individual units, not in groups. The small Shenandoah valley or upland cities are more natural to the eye of the visitor.

A certain traveler starting in to "do" Virginia expressed disappointment, and the doubt whether it had much to appeal. But delving deeper, getting where the people live who made Virginia, this traveler's impressions changed. The final verdict was that few, if any, states had so many points of interest, either of natural or cultural features. The casual traveler is shocked that this country has existed so long without a good road from Mt. Vernon to Washington and thence to the Falls of the Potomac. We seem to be doing the first thing last, but this extensive improvement is hastening on.

The approach to Virginia over the broad, solid, beautiful new bridge of the Potomac is one of the most impressive in the world, viewed from either side. It expresses the breadth of thought, the purpose of unity through acquaintance, the wedding of beauty and strength which are the fit symbols of our beloved central bond. We love Virginia for so much that is noble and beautiful in her past, in her present, and in the prophecy of what she is to become.

The visitor from overseas is greeted on the way to Mount Vernon with the most hideous concatenation of blatant sign boards and catch penny shops that exist anywhere on the broad earth. "Where the carcass is there will the eagles be gathered together," only the eagles are birds of another feather. If Virginia can obliterate this nuisance at her front door she will do the proper and necessary thing. No doubt she will obliterate it, though the action will require heroic measures. The first and the last impression of Virginia ought to be favorable, whether the matter is looked at from the side of dignity and esthetics or from the plain business man's outlook.

Upper Brandon

This mansion of brick, very extensive, was not built until after 1800. William Byrd Harrison erected and developed it. It is now owned by Francis Otway Byrd.

Our pictures (pages 13, 35, 112, 158 and 212) illustrate it as largely as possible. The garden has long reaches of green sward. It is bordered by box in the manner most pleasing to the author at least, because the box does not monopolize too much space, but gains its effect through wider openings. The portraits in the dining room and the adjoining room are particularly pleasing.

One of the most interesting things about the place is that it is still kept up as a great plantation, under the management of the owner who is fond of conducting the enterprise, and has at this very time seven hundred acres in crops. Most of the Virginia estates have become mere retreats for persons of leisure, and therefore they have an air of unnaturalness, being based upon external interests. To find a plantation, therefore, that is still a plantation, adapting itself to modern methods, gives the old sense of being the physical basis of life, just as such places were in Washington's day. They were not play farms or show farms, but supplied the wealth of the owner.

VIRGINIA WATERS

THE ORANGERY RUINS, MT. AIRY

THE JOSHUA FRYE HOUSE

THIS house is of moderate size, and of no remarkable merit, except as it shows an excellent type and is connected historically with interesting characters. (See next page.)

Col. Joshua Frye had Washington under him as a young officer. Washington paid him high compliments for his character and abilities. It is quite probable that in Washington's formative period he acquired from Frye something of the sturdy, steady virtues of that officer, as quoted on the state marker.

When we pass to the house, however, we find twin buttressed chimneys about sixteen feet wide at the base, which width is retained past the ground floor fireplaces. The chimneys then narrow to supply each one fireplace on the second floor. The novice will probably miss the point that there are two side by side fireplaces, one in the front, one in the back room where the chimney is wide, and that this remarkable arrangement is possibly represented by only one instance in the North, the Eleazar Arnold house in Rhode Island. The arrangement is rare even in the South, the usual scheme giving two wholly separate chimneys. The desire for balance and symmetry in nearly all the early houses is strongly in evidence, and that this desire was based on good taste is clear by comparison of the results with the few instances in which a single chimney at one end was opposed by two chimneys at the opposite end.

One may safely recommend A Virginia Switchback (page 209) as something nearly approaching Western scenery. We are bound to say however that this, in the vicinity of Roanoke, is superior, in that one looks down upon the very tops of the apple trees and also observes clusters of farm buildings here and there. Of course a true switchback there is not, but since the sharply sinuous road has that appearance we adopt the name. This is the best of Virginia,—culture features in the midst of natural features.

Westover

Probably this place has been more seen and written about than any other in Virginia, aside of course from Mt. Vernon and Monticello. Before the havoc wrought in the house by the war, when the beautiful low wings matched one another, the residence must have been far handsomer than it is now. The beauty of its great trees (pages 23, 77, 79, 113 and 224)

A ST. PAUL BEND   WAKEFIELD BANKS

OVER THE LEDGES, RUSSELL COUNTY

BENN'S CHURCH, 1632

SABINE HALL GARDEN, RICHMOND COUNTY

BRANDON LAWN

SEVEN OAKS

GENERAL GILBERT'S PLACE, NEAR DANVILLE

BULL RUN BANKS

especially of one vast specimen, and the carefully kept premises, add very greatly to the beauty of the house. Visiting presidents are invited to plant memorial trees.

The garden side, which we also show, is more unusual and its fine iron-work fence, surmounted by carved eagles, assists very much in the composition. The picture called "An Escape Refuge" shows on the left a low roof which covers what is apparently a great well, but is in fact one of the avenues to underground tunnels leading to the house and the river. How this was masked from attackers is not now evident but the opening might have been covered and the place used as a smoke house.

Westover passed out of the hands of the Byrd family about the close of the eighteenth century. The widow of Col. William Byrd III was not able to hold the encumbered estate intact. The second of the line had built the house in the early years of the eighteenth century. The story of the Byrd family is romantic, and otherwise full of interest. This volume, however, not being historical, we merely call attention to the fact that the present generation of Byrds have several outstanding men, one the gentleman of fine suavity, and excellent abilities, who owns Upper Brandon, one the former governor of Virginia and the foremost horticulturalist of the Shenandoah Valley where his orchards extend to hundreds of thousands of trees, and one the explorer whose achievements have been lately so widely honored. The most interesting and cheering feature of all this is that though the family has been distinguished for its capacity, shown in scholarship, in politics, and in social life for many generations, the last generation became the most distinguished of all. Nothing is farther from the fact than the prevalent notion that great men spring from nothing. Capacity is inherited. If self control rules the generations there is no reason why families of great name, from their abilities, should not go on steadily through the generations to higher achievements.

Westover has not now of course the exquisite early furniture that it once boasted. With modest restorations however, it might become what it was regarded even in old days, the most beautiful estate on the James if not in Virginia. It is in the hands of people who are able to bring these things about.

THE NATIONAL FORESTS

FOREST districts set aside as parks by the national government form a very respectable area in Virginia. The proximity of Washington favors such projects, as also that in connection with Williamsburg-Yorktown-Jamestown. One should understand forest in this connection more in the Latin than in the English sense. That is, an outside district, more or less wild, and not necessarily wholly or even mostly covered by trees.

Thus the Natural Bridge district of course includes roads and farms and parcels of land left in private ownership. The government is able to prevent, in one way or another, the bringing of objectionable features into the limits of the forest. The natural resources are conserved; the timber is cut only by way of keeping the forest in prime condition.

Roads are constructed from time to time as appropriations are secured, and probably private rights may gradually be extinguished in the process of the generations.

The Natural Bridge is under private management, and well conducted. No doubt any attempted destruction of fine natural features there or elsewhere would be resisted by the government.

The West, owing to the marvelous natural features like the Yellowstone, the Yosemite and so forth, has in the past properly received greater attention from the government, in the way of securing national ownership than the East. But the greater populations in the East are now receiving attention, since parks within a few hundred miles are of so much more practical value than those that are thousands of miles away. Thus the park taking its name from the Natural Bridge has been made to extend many miles north of that wonderful phenomenon, nearly to Waynesboro.

In the southwest is a region set apart, beginning at Ivanhoe in Wythe County and extending in a long reach into Tennessee.

The Shenandoah National Forest is, in minor part, in West Virginia. It begins in Bath County and runs northeast to Strasburg, not many miles south of Winchester. It is now proposed to add to these forests what is to be called the Shenandoah National Park, extending from Waynesboro northeast to Front Royal and including the Blue Ridge as the Shenandoah Forest includes the Alleghanies. It should be understood that the shapes and directions of these reservations are based on the mountain ranges. The area included is largely land too high or rough to serve for agriculture, and

SHENANDOAH COUNTY POOL

HOT SPRINGS FARMSTEAD

KITCHEN AND SMOKE HOUSE, STRATFORD

DRAWING ROOM, BRANDON

will not therefore subtract markedly from the productive capacity of the state. The largest natural resource in the reservations is the timber.

Sometimes we hesitate to provide far enough in the future. Now it may seem a vast area to segregate and pay for. But fifty years from now the grandchildren will bless us for every square mile thus forever secured to beauty and incidentally to hold the rainfall and prevent destructive freshets. The beauties of these districts are mostly in the mountain contours, and the silences of forest seclusion.

Two or three roads in this region we show. Camping, under wise restrictions, thus permitting long vacations among these mountain glories, is feasible.

In addition to Washington, Baltimore and Richmond and lesser populations near at hand, east of the mountains, we may well note that the great and populous state of Ohio, in a plains country, is not far away, and will have benefits arising from its nearness.

These reservations form the only mountain districts till we cross the entire Mississippi basin and reach the Rocky Mountains.

With the rapidly developing means of moving about, these mountain parks, for such would be a proper name for them, are nearer our front door than the next county was a hundred years ago.

A SUFFOLK HOMESTEAD

OWING to several fires Suffolk cannot show us the dwellings of the settlers. But settlement here was almost as early as anywhere in America.

We show one house, a solid brick four chimney, wide spreading dwelling, with its half windows under the eaves, and its tying brick wing between the chimneys—always a pleasing and solid device. The style came in about 1800. It secured amplitude, comfort, and gave a hint of the generous host, the solid citizen who built it.

The vicinity of Suffolk afforded, on its tidal river, one of the most prized and most used harbors of the primitive time.

The new route across the bridge of the James is putting Suffolk to the fore as a visitation point, easily taken in with Portsmouth and Norfolk. It is a region where much beautiful furniture has been preserved or brought in from the plantations.

It is on the natural shore route south, an introduction to that vast

lowland country rich in culture for northern markets, or stretching in watery wastes, the abode of water fowl, the nursery of the cypress, as one stretches away for the tidewater reaches of North Carolina. It affords a good late fall and early spring alternate route, and is a revelation of that great American Holland which will one day redeem still more of its acres and become the garden of the East.

The Lordly James (page 176) is a scene that opens to us on the way toward the Natural Bridge from Lynchburg. I believe it is the only picture ever made by me showing a railway. The magnificence however of this valley regarded either from the east as here or from the west on the slopes of the Blue Ridge is such that it remains in memory with the impression that it is preëminent in its way. The broad plain dotted with farm houses and decorated with foliage, the sweep of the great stream confident of its power, and placid in movement, the fair and mysterious crests that repose on the sky line are but a few of the beauties that appeal to one.

Brandon

On the south side of the James this famous residence, which we illustrate quite largely (pages 14, 24, 25, 55, 149, 158, 163) is similar in its

TALLWOOD HOUSE

CLAREMONT FRONT

UPPER BRANDON DINING ROOM

UPPER BRANDON LAWN

elevation above the James to that of Westover. The banks rise to a considerable degree, leaving a good many of these sites sufficiently above the water level to attain a moderate outlook, and to secure thoroughly dry cellars. Brandon also is very celebrated for its garden. The principal turf walk to the river, which in this case is the garden side, terminates in a rich garden ornament. There is in these grounds a pecan tree of such dimensions of trunk, height and spread as perhaps to make it unique among the trees of its kind. There is no edifice near it to emphasize this magnificence, which is sufficient to dwarf the largest residence in Virginia. The plan of the house makes more of the wings than usual. Although the building suffered in the war, the damage is repaired. The hall and its adjacent rooms are of great beauty and spaciousness. The title to Brandon goes back to the earliest time. In the first transfer it came to a brother-in-law of Shakespeare's daughter, after that it came into the Harrison family, which has furnished us two presidents. Brandon from its location is somewhat more secluded than the opposite side of the river. Its charming gardens are appealing from their extent and the wonderful variety extending from the rose to the mightiest of trees. It might easily be said that no more attractive retreat exists in Virginia.

The house was built early in the eighteenth century, namely in the Queen Anne time and has much handsome paneling. Externally it has not as much pretension to height or massiveness as some other Virginia places. Its extent, however, is broad. It has a warm and homelike atmosphere without and within. The portraits in particular, especially those of youthful persons, have a delightfully graceful aspect, relieving the residence from that cold mustiness so often characteristic of ancient homes. The interior is perhaps favorable to more good pictorial effects than almost any other place we have seen.

This place has recently passed into the hands of Mr. Robert W. Daniel.

A SALEM GABLE ENDER

AS WE passed through old Salem we found this dwelling was about to be torn down. While it is not unique it is rare in the south and meritorious anywhere.

For many years it has been used as a tobacco warehouse but of course

160

must originally have been a residence owing to its four end chimneys. The period is not very early. We find the styles as late as 1830 and perhaps never earlier than 1790. The sharp pitched roof is an excellent reversion to 1760 and earlier, after a long continued style, from the Revolution to 1825, of a low pitched hip roof, not sufficient to shed water well, but suggested by the classical style, which men should have remembered flourished in a region where snow almost never fell, or fell lightly.

These houses afforded fine third story rooms with good windows without dormers. They were therefore practical and avoided many expensive features which did not stand the weather. The dormer is a beautiful detail but necessitates heavy initial cost and frequent subsequent attention. It is interesting therefore to see how the practical builders of the early nineteenth century met the matter.

The erection of chimneys in the outer wall afforded more room within than other schemes, and when the gable occurred at the chimney ends it was also possible to provide heat in the third story. The scheme of two chimneys, between the front and back rooms gave four fireplaces but cut the house into separated quarters on each floor.

The roof construction of this house gave better rooms on the third floor, but actually lessened the expense of construction. It also provided a house which when slated was practically fire proof from external danger.

Where Would One Live?

One of the outstanding pleasures of traveling about a state is the continuous occupation of selecting a residence. We do not mean that one should forsake the home of his fathers, except for one far better. But it is an unmeasured delight to arrange these things in the imagination, to select the slope, the setting to be occupied by the house, or to take such a house already existing and give it back its original perfections. Should one be eager to enter into this game in which there is everything to win, we suggest the vicinity of Wytheville. East or south of Lynchburg is another fruitful region in suggestion, and we have already pointed out the merits that appeal to one in the extreme southwest. Loudoun County and vicinity of Leesburg being near the Potomac and Washington, and possessing distinction of its own, is another focus of interest. Roanoke, on the slopes of either range, might furnish a site beautiful in itself and convenient to an agreeable center. Without mentioning again a number of delectable neighborhoods, we were attracted to the region about Halifax in the county of

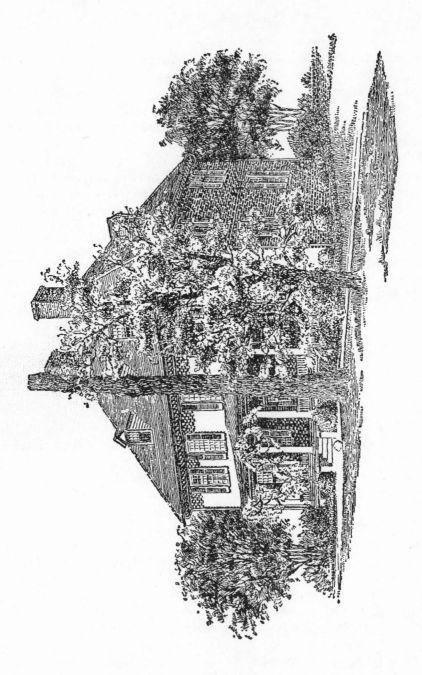

MANTEL AND FESTOON

DINING ROOM, BRANDON

SARATOGA BETWEEN DOGWOOD BLOSSOMS

THREE GABLES

the same name, of Appomattox with its softly rolling slopes. In the Tidewater the south side of the James has not become so famous as the opposite side and therefore affords, perhaps, more attractive sites for development. The region near Washington is that being principally taken up for country residences, as is natural. The neighborhood of Gunston Hall, of Fairfax, and of Warrenton has each its peculiar charm. If it is an independent country place without reference to cities, one would say that the slopes of the Appalachians around the various springs are the finest regions for the development of a really fine country place. Yet humanity, especially that part of it that loves books, is always harking back to the historic, so that the person who loves rural conditions and the vicinity of a great past should be very happy in one of many sites on the Northern Neck.

THE PRESIDENT'S HOUSE, WILLIAMSBURG

BUILT up again after an accidental burning when used as quarters by the French in the Revolution, this house with its opposite twin, the Indian school, forms the introduction to the greater edifices of William and Mary College, an institution peculiar in that while it has great age it is within this generation taking on a sudden lusty growth so that instead of being merely an historic relic it is the teeming mother of a great institution where rank on rank of edifices rise, where students gather from every quarter in impressive numbers. (See page 162.)

The favorite black and red brick in Flemish bond, which occurs generally over the oldest South, is seen here in early examples.

The main central edifice of the college, seen between this house and its opposite neighbor, is undergoing restoration and the reproduction of the copper plate of it is shown in this volume. I remarked how unfortunate it was that a wooden cornice should be placed on this edifice, and on the next visit, about a month after, I found a similar cornice on a neighboring building had been swept by fire.

It is understood that Mrs. Rockefeller is much interested in the College which has of late grown, both in dormitories and occupants, far faster than the town. Williamsburg will soon find itself under the necessity of taking care lest it lose its village charm by getting too large.

The magnitude of the work here, the restoration of an entire little city, has been so made known that people gather from every quarter. We hope not too many may come, nor too much of a modern tone take possession.

Mount Airy

The estate of Mt. Airy in Richmond County, is in the thought of many of us, the most beautiful in all Virginia, and if we go beyond the bounds of Virginia, it is a question where we should find another place to match it. The location is the first merit which immediately impresses us. It has the elevation and general attractiveness of site that is so notable a feature in the distant Piedmont section. It lies a mile or two back from the Rappahannock, and is only a few miles from Wakefield on the Potomac. Of course the estate extended to the river on the Rappahannock side. It has, therefore, all the advantage of the fine air and outlook of the upper country together with the boundary on Tidewater, a matter of the highest importance when all the freight was water borne.

The next impressive feature is that the edifice is of stone. This indicates a strong feeling for solidity and a desire to imitate the more solid country houses of England. The coigns and other trim in white stone are finely contrasted with the brown tints which form the principal part of the wall. The crowning feature of merit is, however, the general design by which the central building is connected by curtain structures of one story, serving as passages and curving back, to the handsome subordinate wings. The whole seems to have been built at one time and very carefully carried out. One wing was reserved for guests, while another was the service end of the premises. On the side of the public entrance a natural terrace drops away to the park which is beautifully wooded, in that open exquisite fashion which allows each tree to develop its individuality and obtain its strength without constriction as it sends out its mighty limbs in every direction. The garden side is that away from which the wings sweep. The ruins of the orangery at just the right distance to be interesting without being obtrusive give with their massive brick arches an old world effect, especially as they are fronted with box, which again lies behind a willow whose long draperies sway gently in front of the old arches (pages 118 and 144). On the slope at the other end of the group of buildings are some cedars, one of which we found to be seventeen feet in circumference at the height of one's shoulder. The mighty boles of scattered sycamore trees are also found on the garden front.

This estate has for many generations been in the Tayloe family, who

FALLING SPRINGS ROAD

BOX MAZE, JEFFERSON'S SCHOOL, TUCKAHOE

FLAGS AND ROSES

still hold it. A fire in the nineteenth century destroyed much of the original paneling which, however, was restored, and the exterior remained intact. The great central hall is not merely a passage but, from its location and amplitude and splendid lighting, has always been the natural gathering place of the family. The sweet old Virginia spirit still presides here and the courage and persistency to carry everything forward on the old lines in the family tradition.

The place was built in the heyday of the eighteenth century, in 1758. Even so it was not the first house. That had been located like other Virginia plantations on the lower ground near the Tidewater. Evidently a great light dawned on Col. John Tayloe else he would not have abandoned the solid original dwelling. Even in those days it must have been observed that the higher lands were conducive to health. He not only carried through the erection which we have mentioned but made balustraded approaches and stairs, and completed the effectiveness of all by grass plots filling the approaches.

The casual student of history who speaks of the early days as crude or primitive has much to learn in Virginia in general and from Mt. Airy in particular. There was an opulence in life in that day which is scarcely equaled in the most luxurious mansions of the present, because there was an amplitude about the old life that allowed one to see it and feel it at leisure. Books, art, good company, good living were based upon the best traditions of English country life and were sustained by the unequaled natural resources of many thousands of broad acres, rich in culture and backed by forests of walnut and oak. When you combine in your thought a place like Mt. Airy with hundreds of other plantations some of them as richly endowed, and all of them replete with commercial products, it is not to be wondered at that Richmond and Westmoreland counties could gather a body of gentlemen who in their capacity of mind, in their breadth of view, and in their dress and equipage and residences, could bear comparison often to their own advantage with the English country life from which they came. It is true they had no roads worthy of the name, but neither had they in England. But so great was the superiority of the water communications here, that planters might often visit each other, conveyed in their handsome barges as well turned out, and as gracefully fitted to meet their world as we could be on our stone roads. Furthermore they had the advantage in living in an age when fine taste predominated in structures and decorations, and when horseback riding tended to that exhilaration of health and that easy poise of manner which in all generations and in every country has characterized the cavalier.

Tallwood House (page 157) is attractive from its symmetry though the date is not very early. It is the only example which we have seen of a house with four so called cathedral chimneys, each one with a series of four arches. A house derives great beauty from such ornamentation, and there is the soundest possible reason for building protected flues, in this or some other manner. Such flues keep the chimneys dry; also, their protected tops prevent a down draught. It is a mystery why all chimneys are not built either in this manner or at least with square caps in which are openings.

Tallwood, presumably, derived its name from the magnificent height of the trees in the grounds. There is here also a remarkable yew and a fine garden with beautifully covered pergolas.

Stratford

The recent acquisition of Stratford and its imminent restoration in a large way so as to include magnificent gardens has called the public attention again to the perhaps unrivaled number in successive generations of men who have rendered the Lee family illustrious. The purchase of the property has included very broad lands so that the original approach from the river may be restored, and the thickening growths so far cleared as to provide again a broad outlook. The details concerning this great house and the Lee family are so fully public property that it is unnecessary to enter into them with any degree of fullness. It is perhaps sufficient to say to justify the sentiment for restoration, that General Robert E. Lee was born here and that he desired to return here and spend his last years. This desire he was personally unable to carry out, although in retrospect it seems strange that his friends did not band together to accomplish his wish at a time when the property was held at a low figure. But this easy wisdom after the event need not hinder the present powerful interests which will shortly carry to a very satisfactory termination the establishment of the estate as a permanent memorial to General Lee and his family. It is understood that already one person has offered to bear all of the expense, but that it has been thought better for many to have a part in this effort.

The edifice itself will not require any such restoration as will change its present lines except so far as the entrance stair is concerned. A considerable number of the out buildings in solid brick are also in a fair degree of preservation. The kitchen in particular, with its huge fireplace, is typical of the

A MONTPELIER BORDER

THE LAWN TEMPLE, MONTPELIER

THE ST. PAUL DRIVE

BY THE LEE HIGHWAY

great plantation life.   One small brick structure is thought, perhaps, to have served as a school at one time.   The most impressive immediate beauty about the place is the wonderful beech trees with their tangled roots like the drawings of a Doré.

Inside the residence, the bedroom which was the birthplace of the great general and some of his ancestors, is known.   The great central assembly hall completely paneled, is impressive, and so is the wide extent and ample height of the basement.   The chimney formation we have already referred to.

As old as this place is it follows another still older destroyed shortly after its completion.   The great respect in which Col. Thomas Lee was held, is testified by the fact that the English government recognized his services in a substantial manner.   His loss from the fire would seem a great sum even at the present day.   When this dwelling, with its unique architecture and its excellent setting, all serving to gather up the long and celebrated succession of great men, is completed, in the midst of broad gardens overlooking its river, neighboring other great estates, and convenient to the national capital, it will form, we would say, one of the outstanding trio of Virginia, the other two being Mt. Vernon and Monticello.   The pictures are on pages 45, 46 and 154.

THE HOUSES OF VIRGINIA

THAT the Virginians built the finest houses in our country in the old time, is accounted for by several causes, one of which is that they had the funds to pay for such houses.   It has been said that Washington was the wealthiest man in the colonies, by what warrant I know not, for probably such men as Robert Morris were wealthier.   He was, however, by the standards of the day, wealthy, and one of many planters able to have a house comparable in style and extent with those on the great English estates.

In fact there were only three directions in which to expend money in those days, in gambling, which afforded an adequate outlet for any income, investment in "western" lands, and in building fine dwellings.   In all these directions the planters, therefore, moved.   The more sagacious like Washington, restricted their bets within compass.   Many, however, like him, bought heavily the lands in the parts of the state, and beyond, not yet settled.

Students have wondered at the heavy expenditures for building and even for many luxuries by settlers, north and south, even as early as the seventeenth century. To us, thinking of the great undeveloped country back from the shore fringe, it seems strange indeed to read the inventories of the old estates, rich in silver, napery, furniture, carriages, and raiment, until the lists make us feel, what is the fact, that we are at the unlading of a ship from London, heavy with the latest and richest products of that world metropolis, ordered by successful planters, who desired their families to have such habitations and habiliments as might comport with the best society of the age.

Those old worthies did not wholly envision the developments to come in America. Nobody did. But they nearly all invested as heavily as their fortunes allowed in lands to the west of them. They bought enough to provide richly for the generations to come.

Regarding their dwellings however their feeling was one of unity with the home country and they felt secure from attack. They came to America to better their condition. At least that was one of the reasons. They were ambitious in having excellent dwellings. Service was cheap. Bricks could be made at a low figure. Timber, and that the best, was super-abundant. They must either build with it or burn it. Stone, found usually as limestone was more difficult to quarry and draw. Hence we find that brick, made on or near the plantation, or wood were the ordinary materials. Jefferson complains with some bitterness of the absence of good architecture, and particularly that durable materials were not used. When we consider the number of substantial planters and the comparatively small number of good houses they built we may agree with him. It is also possible that Jefferson, whose taste was largely framed on classical models and who had spent much time on the continent, did not feel so much as we do the importance and beauty of the Georgian style. At least he seems to have made little use of it in the many beautiful erections he inspired or directly ordered.

The woods available for building were oak, walnut, tulip, pine. Many other woods were employed occasionally, as sycamore, but such was the abundance and the merit of this great quartet that there was little reason to seek farther.

The magnificence of the oaks of Virginia is the most striking feature wherever they have been long unmolested. Old oaks in England are almost invariably short of stem. Their boles scarcely afford a single length

FALLING SPRINGS CASCADE

SPRING BY THE RIVER   BLACKBERRY BLOSSOM BROOK

THE LORDLY JAMES

of log. At an early period builders looked beyond English shores for oak, at least across the narrow seas to Ireland. But in Virginia even now one sees many oaks looming skyward, straight as an arrow, capable of affording a sixty foot cut without a knot. To just what proportion the use of oak in frames extended I have been unable to ascertain, but it is probable that as in the north, woods easier to work soon superseded the oak. Paneling in particular, of oak, is extremely rare in America, though it is found, as well as mahogany. Pine is usual, but in a good number of fine houses walnut was used for this purpose, as easily taking a rich finish, and was also used even in framing. No doubt England profited heavily by importing Virginia walnut which was in the height of fashion for finish and especially for furniture from the late seventeenth till near the middle of the eighteenth century, at just the time when it was most abundant in Virginia, and when the planters were themselves using it.

A fine house at Chelsea is in walnut paneling, but was until this very season supposed to be in pine, since it was painted white. The owner accidentally discovered what was beneath the surface. No doubt other similar finds will be made.

Walnut is an easy wood to work, at least in such knotless timbers as were available here, and the wonder might be that it was not quite general in paneling. The fashion of painting, however, made the material underneath of small importance. The desire for light in the rooms, testified by the white paint, whether from the merit of the idea or the fashion of the time, ruled the plain walnut out.

The tulip tree, commonly called tulip-poplar in the South, grows to magnificent proportions. It is a semi-soft wood, and very well adapted to carving. Perhaps for this reason it is found in the great fluted pilasters of the hall in the Carter's Grove house, though the paneling is in pine, ridiculously said to be oak in a recent book on Virginia.

Beech is found in Virginia, some trees as at Stratford, the Lee homestead, reaching to noble dimensions. But how general it was I do not know nor whether it was used very much. Of course there are examples in furniture of the Queen Anne time but walnut was so much handsomer that the reason for the use of beech did not exist as in England. There it was the common substitute for the more expensive walnut.

Having then such a wealth of raw materials as the world had never known, all in the clay about, or in the forests pressing their very home lots, having a taste trained by English memories or education, it is not a marvel that the planters built many beautiful houses, but that they did not build more of them. At the present time many wealthy persons throughout the nation, having no taste—for they cannot even be said to have poor taste—dwell in houses which merit the sharp severity of Jefferson's remarks.

It is common to hear remarks about the "primitive" times as if the American settlers lived in a dark age.

Why do men forget that Grinling Gibbons, the greatest English carver who ever lived, was turning out his wonderful work in the late seventeenth and early eighteenth centuries, at the very time when the planters were creating their dwellings? It was the age of the great architects, the high tide of literary production also, and the present day American, in his flimsy gingerbread house, looking down on the "crudeness" of his ancestors, is one of the most pitiable objects imaginable.

The place of the Virginian house was influenced in part by the climate.

Though a kitchen was often provided in the basement, a separate structure wholly removed from the residence or connected with it by a corridor or arcade or curtain wall was common. The name summer kitchen applied to these edifices is sometimes abbreviated to kitchen, because it was perhaps the only kitchen, especially when attached to the house. These kitchens, and indeed the quarters for the servants, are now the most picturesque portions of the establishment, covered as they are with riotous vines which have taken complete possession, or snuggling beneath the spreading trees, and having within vast fireplaces capable of any demand upon them when guests thronged the great house.

The plan of the dwelling was far more varied than superficial attention to the subject might lead us to infer. The central house might or might not be lifted well above a high basement. The nature of the site, whether low or high, may have influenced this detail, but we find some good houses so built that a step or two carries one to the level of the main floor, though the site is low, and again a long flight of approaching steps is required where the site is high. It was a matter regulated more by preference, or by the desire for a series of rooms in a basement which would allow more space above.

Instead then of running an ell back and forming a T shaped plan it was usual on a fine estate to add an ell at each end extending along the main axis of the dwelling, or to interpose a covered way from the main house to such ells on either hand. The advantage of the corridor, arcade or simple one storied narrow connection was three fold. It gave a finer effect of

PARLOR MANTEL, KEIM HOUSE

FALLING SPRING BRANCH

ROSE ARCH, VIRGINIA UNIVERSITY

THE SIAMESE ACCOMAC HOUSE

A THREATENED STORM

A FRONDED CONE

amplitude, as one viewed the house from without; it provided more light at the ends which would otherwise have abutted, and it removed the heat and odor of the cooking on the one end and gave greater seclusion on the other.

Even these subordinate wings were sometimes only one story high, but at times extended to two stories. In the great plantations as at Carter's Hall (to be distinguished from Carter's Grove) there was still another pair of buildings, two stories high, or less, detached or connected and all on the same long axis. The effect was one of much magnificence, since the entire group of buildings was arrayed on a front as extensive as that of the largest English houses. But sometimes as at Shirley the subordinate edifices were placed well away and retracted from the main house. In this case the purpose was obviously to provide a flood of light on all sides without obstruction, and, even in the third story, providing rank on rank of large windows. Whoever built Shirley, and that is a mooted point, evidently loved light or regarded it as essential to health. From three sides of this unique residence fine views of the James may be had.

Of course the bringing of food, if it were to be kept hot, across open or even enclosed cold spaces was a problem. In England the same situation has taught the people to enjoy cold toast, and it is really better cold! But great dishes could be covered, and hot water trenchers with double bottoms were known.

Another scheme of the houses and "offices," (a word of exasperating frequence and varied significance in England) was that of connecting the great house by curving or angling passages with the dependencies, as at Mount Vernon. The effect of this arrangement is charming, but only on the inside curve, the "land front," does the extent of the premises impress one. Indeed Mount Vernon seems directly in front a rather mean, or at least unpretentious abode.

But within the lawn on the land approach the place looks like what it really is, a village of dwellings. This arrangement is good in certain particulars. If there were need to pass from one dependency to another it was a short way across. Again there were supplied two totally differing fronts, for none of these large places had a back side and their present owners would resent such a term, as coming only from inferior persons who knew not the ways of the "quality." Thus a garden on one front and a lawn on the other, together with the two divergent aspects of the house, gave a double charm to the approaches.

There was also the H plan as at Tuckahoe in which the connecting link was a large hall or assembly room, and in other cases merely a passage. The plan of building about three sides of a square was also followed.

Besides all these plans, varied still further by many divergences, there were in the greater places additional buildings for field hands; and all had sheds, barns and particularly separate smoke and ice houses which even to-day are the features on which the eye rests with much pleasure. These last buildings were either circular or square but in either case the roof reached a pinnacle.

Of course garden temples or arcades completed the more extensive premises, while statues or fountains adorned the vistas or the intersections of the walks.

In short it was the aim of the ambitious Virginian and of the South in general, to establish a handsome country place. This aim was achieved. There are almost no places in the North of this character. One thing, however, is seen in the North oftener than in the South, the porter's lodge. This is rare in Virginia because there was no effort to keep people out. Whoever approached a gate had come from far. The mood of the planter as well as the isolation of the plantation called for hospitality. There was no village about the gate, as often in England. Indeed the water front, which was important, it was scarcely possible to fence off from the public, even if the desire to do so had existed.

One marked feature of many great houses, as at Stratford and Monticello, was the removal of the stair from the main hall. Indeed at Monticello there is a cramped hidden stairway. This mistake, for it was a mistake, arose perhaps from following classical memories. At any rate a great square hall without a stair is never attractive unless filled with people. The beauty of a fine stair as seen in a Southern house, is its crowning glory. In fact the stair and the fireplace were the only features easily lending themselves to central decorative themes.. The emphasis on doorheads, often made very handsome, overcame only in small measure the neglect of the stair.

One would say that the most serious error made by the builders of the old houses was their failure to cover them with slate rather than with shingles. We know that some of the earliest cottages were thatched. That, however, was probably never true of any of the great houses. The mellow effect of old slate, which in this climate is practically indestructible, would have been the crowning glory of the house. The explanation of this

ALONG THE PICKET FENCE

A VIRGINIA FOREST DRIVE

WYTHEVILLE GATES

THE PLACID ROANOKE

failure to use slate is difficult to explain, because expense did not stop the planter.

———————

It is here and there possible to buy a famous old plantation. Several of such were called to our attention. The voice of the realtor is heard in the land. Whether you wish one of the sweet water nooks around Irvington, Readsville, and the outer end of the Neck, or a home on the upland ridge amid the abundant laurel, you may satisfy yourself.

Of course the great city, without a rival, as a residence is Richmond. The small city, before one turns towards the mountains, is Fredericksburg. The valley cities are Winchester, Harrisonburg, and Staunton. The valley villages are Woodstock, Strasburg (or is this a city?) and Berryville. Of course when we mention any of these places we do not refer to their centers but to their circumferences.

A TYPICAL VIRGINIAN HOUSE

ALTHOUGH we mentioned first the great house it was not the most important. The typical dwelling, based on the small English manor house, existed in such great numbers as to outweigh the more pretentious erections.

And let no one mistake by overlooking this smaller typical dwelling, even though it consisted, downstairs, of two rooms only. The perfect balance, the nice proportions, the inherent beauty and obvious perfection of plan and aptness for purpose which marks this house renders it intensely interesting.

The material was wood, or in the better specimens brick. The first outstanding feature was the chimney arrangement. A chimney rising from either end charmingly punctuated the landscape and warmed one's heart, even as such a dwelling came in sight. The chimney of this typical dwelling was built outside the house and began with a very broad base, reaching now and then to sixteen feet, in order to afford a generous fireplace. As the chimney rose it narrowed, buttress like, once as it passed the main fireplace, and again as it passed the smaller one in the chamber. At this point an odd constructive feature intervened, possibly occurring in

187

England, but not to the writer's recollection. The whole depth of the fireplace being in the external chimney, the final stack above it, not requiring the full size, was built on a line with the outside edge of the masonry wholly free of the house itself. The advantage was escape from the heat of the chimney, often not wanted, and escape from the expensive structural work and flashing about the gable. At first sight one is so surprised by this construction that he questions its taste and harmony. But after seeing thousands of such chimneys one begins to feel their absolute adaptation.

The main door is flanked by two or three windows in the rooms on each side of the "passage" as the hall is often called. A gabled portico without pillars, but like an enlarged window cap, may top the door, and the house often has only one full story, the sharply slanted roof (always so for beauty and room) being pierced by five or more uniform dormers. That is all there is. It is enough. One may study endlessly, but to increase the beauty of this construction is impossible. Make it more decorative and it is less beautiful.

There are extensions of the idea, like running the walls up two full stories, and still keeping the dormers on the third. This of course adds much to the dignity of the dwelling. The chimneys also being heightened, and allowing of one more set back, become almost imposing. When a dwelling reaches these dimensions an ell is sometimes added at the back as in the Frye house, but a free movement of air through the passage is thereby lost. Another variant of the plan allows four rooms below. If the walls are two full stories, the rear roof may be carried down to cover a two-room-deep ground floor. This secures the leanto effect. Of course, then, a second chimney is required at each end, but it is subordinate in height to the chimney in front of it.

The carrying out of a full eight room and attic plan affords twin chimneys, identical, at each end of the house and lifts it to the plan if not to the proportions of the central "great" house. Dwellings of the simpler character either had basement kitchens and even other basement rooms, or were served from small detached kitchens.

It was a favorite scheme to build an apparently one story house, where the land sloped away on the garden side, and afforded a full basement for dining room and kitchen. The dormer windows gave upstairs rooms and thus a very snug little place like the Warren house, sometimes called the Rolfe house, really afforded a full amount of room.

AN APPALACHIAN VALLEY

POWELL'S RIVER BANKS

CANAL BOAT NEAR HARPER'S FERRY

AN "AIRPLANE" OUTLOOK ABOVE ROANOKE

VIRGINIA BEAUTIFUL

A favorite method in simple dwellings was to recess the central part of the main floor, for nearly half the length of the house, in the rear, affording a covered porch into which three rooms gave. In the course of this small work we shall show other plans, some surprisingly attractive, as the Accomac Siamese house.

One is struck in Pennsylvania and so on South, by the large number of excellent log houses, some of quite ample proportions, still standing and often kept up in the pink of condition and with obvious pride in the quaint old time.

The author was asked by the late Dr. Mercer, of Doylestown, to be informed about the log house of New England. He expressed much surprise that none seemed to remain, except in the remotest backwoods. Such however is the fact. The ancient house at Exeter where Daniel Webster boarded as a student has been found to be of squared logs under the clapboards. It is a very rare example and even so the squared timbers take it, precisely speaking, out of the class, occurring to the writer, north of Pennsylvania, of a well kept up log house.

In Virginia it is no uncommon thing to see a dwelling of logs the corners of which are dovetailed together, almost with the nicety of cabinet work, and every part of the edifice as carefully constructed as if for the mansion of a man of means. These houses are very charming with their neatly whitewashed or even painted walls. The interspaces of the logs are carefully chinked with plaster. Within, where the idea of permanence is carried out, the wall may also be furred and plastered or covered with wainscot sheathing.

The chimneys of such dwellings being commonly of stone the effect is most pleasing. Some such houses are limited to the one room class, with a chimney at one end. Others are double with the two end chimneys and even with dormers and simple porches.

In this very year the writer observed several new houses of this character, in process of erection. Of course they are a luxury, on account of the large amount of lumber employed, except at points well away from a market.

But the tobacco drying barns of southern central Virginia are practically all built of logs and some are covered with the early type of long shaved shingles.

The roof lines of Virginia are an endless source of beauty and delight, disclosing themselves as one journeys through the country.

BENN'S CHURCH

NOT far from Suffolk, and near to the south end of the great bridge over the James centered just north of Newport News, and close by Smithfield, is a church edifice set in the midst of forest trees as companions. The trees are singularly beautiful and the church is back among them, and retired a good deal from the main road. Here among the softly rustling leaves, the chattering of the squirrel and the songs of the mocking bird, but far from the roar of modern life, reposes this church, regarded as the oldest edifice in English construction, certainly the oldest church in our country. Some of the bricks are said to bear out the date claimed, 1632. This makes the Ship Church in Hingham, Massachusetts, a very much younger sister.

There is a striking similarity between the tower here and the ruinous tower of the Jamestown church. They both apparently reach back to the time when no American type had come into existence, for they copy the main features of the English parish church. Such restorations as were necessary have been made by the devotion of architect and donors. There is no spot sweeter, none with a stronger flavor of the very ancient American day than this. Two pictures are shown (pages 40 and 148). The church key is at the neighboring shop, but the chief interest is the exterior.

LONG BRANCH

IN CLARKE COUNTY where so many noble homes were centers of the best Virginia life this one is also found, of a date in the first decade of the nineteenth century, when the columnar fronts, not found much earlier, were rapidly becoming the vogue. We refer more particularly to the great round columns, often fluted, which were preceded by the smaller pillars, often square, as at Mt. Vernon.

The grounds abound with magnificent trees, such as the best estates of Virginia nearly always possessed. Indeed, here as in England, a country estate without a parklike approach was considered quite out of the question.

The dwelling is of brick, square, with a hip roof of moderate pitch and four chimneys, such a house as became so general among the well to do all over the nation, from the close of the Revolution to 1820. There is a large

VIRGINIA ANGLES

CREST OF THE PASS

MOUNTAIN FARM ROAD

LEXINGTON AND THE ALLEGHANIES

HOUSE MOUNTAIN, FROM LEXINGTON

A MOUNTAIN NEST

glazed outlook on the roof, with views of the fair farm lands of the county, particularly of the meadows of this farm far below graced by sycamores of vast size and grazed over by the home flock, as shown in another of the pictures—a perfect pastoral outlook.

Curiously the one storied ell of the dwelling is battlemented, one surmises to retain in the low roof effect, the windows in the main house overlooking this ell. Service quarters carry the structure still farther out.

The location, facing on the one hand the grove, on the other hand the valley, is among the most attractive in the state.

HOUSE OF DANIEL MORGAN

THIS Winchester dwelling is called after General Morgan the hero of the battle of Cowpens, and he is said to have died in this house in 1802. The bay window on the front would not then, presumably, be original. It was a fine town house for its day, but made no pretension to be in the first rank. Morgan was a favorite, and deservedly so, of Washington. After the war the generals of the Revolution scattered, and according to their ability, from Maine to Georgia, took up lands on the frontier or settled, like Morgan, on the inner line of the new country. Some of them had been impoverished by the war. Land grants were a favorite form of settlement with the soldiers of all ranks.

Many early features at Winchester claim attention, but some have been much illustrated previously, as Washington's headquarters, and many will be specially noted.

It should be understood that some edifices are so buried in foliage that it is not practicable to illustrate them. Others have been so marred by bad additions as to be unworthy of illustration in spite of their original merit or historic associations. The author has tried to follow the middle course so as not to show dwellings too degenerate.

It is a favorite remark in showing houses of brick in America to say that the brick came from England. While this is sometimes possible it is seldom probable, and is never important. The phrase English brick was often used to denote the size. That is to say bricks were made in more than one size in this country. The use of the phrase is analogous with the phrases English bond and Flemish bond.

CRAB APPLE ORCHARD FORT

Especially in the case of a dwelling removed a good number of miles from navigable water, it is an absurdity to presume that the bricks were English, since their carriage would have cost more than the bricks themselves. The heavy freights went from America to England, except in the case of tobacco. The English ships on their return cargoes might sometimes have brought bricks as ballast if their cargos were light, and the bricks would be used near the place of the landing.

One will often have work pointed out in these dwellings as hand carving. What other sort of carving was there? Even today the best shops confine themselves to hand carving, and it is only very recently that any other method was possible.

In the tobacco raising districts of Virginia there is a general lack of cities and there are comparatively few fine planters' residences. The base of Virginia bordering on North Carolina and Tennessee is more than four hun-

THE LEANTO HOUSE

GARDEN BORDER, CLAREMONT

MONTPELIER TERRACES

WYTHE HOUSE, WILLIAMSBURG

dred miles in length. About half of this distance is Tidewater, and from the Roanoke River to the sea there are in the southern counties only three places marked on state maps as being notably good dwellings. The distance from Tidewater was too great to render any crops profitable. The development since the war of 1861–65 is to be depended upon to bring this region into greater affluence, so that its people may take advantage of the revival of good architecture. One imagines that the improved transportation of the last decade will do more for this part of Virginia than for any other section.

SUCCESSION IN GARDENS

HUMAN ingenuity may strive as it will but gardens will always be most beautiful in the spring. The iris or the lily, and the poppy, followed by the rose and the peony, and at last by the larkspur and the hollyhock, all run their rapid course in Virginia and are gone much sooner than in the North. The author is never satisfied with a garden that does not contain many large shrubs and even some trees to give it diversity. Some of the notable gardens of Virginia have lost nearly all their beauty by the beginning of summer. We presume that most owners frankly face the difficulty of continuation of blossoms and do not attempt it. The climate of summer induces one to keep to the shaded rooms or porches. The Virginian does not need a summer garden as much as the dwellers in the severer climates.

Still one remembers that even in a presumably hot climate, Adam was found in the cool of the day in a garden. We are, however, allowed to believe, or at least to hope, that there were no intrusive insects in Adam's garden. The early morning is the glory of the day. Consequently the best of the world is practically unseen, for every one person who is about, breathing in the freshness of the dawn, a thousand are still snuggling in dreamland.

One notices of late an effort to establish rock gardens with pools. These of course owing to their pleasing variety, contrast, and coolness, are much to be desired wherever water is available. One can remember, however, not more than one such feature in fifty gardens. By rights there should be an irregularity of surface. Aquatic plants like the water lily, and flowering river grasses, treble the beauty and joy derivable from a garden.

No garden is complete without walls or low buildings or the proximity

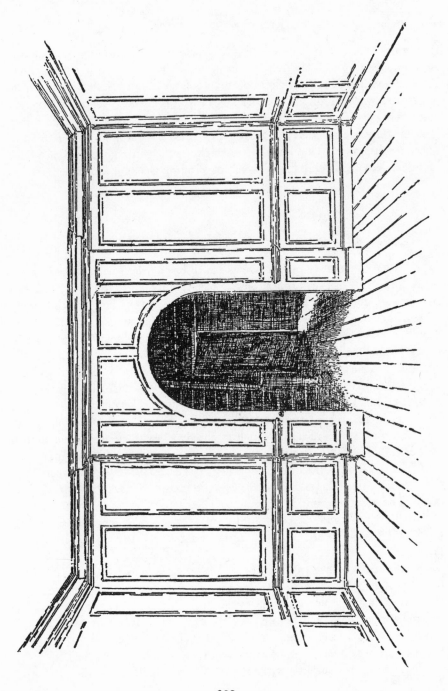

of the ell of the dwelling to form a background for the tall stalks of the yucca
or the hollyhock and larkspur, which are never good planted out like rows
of corn.   Some small edifice in a garden, in addition to an arbor, adds to its
coziness and charm and sense of intimacy.

VIRGINIA BEAUTIFUL

Tuckahoe

The date of this house, like that of most others, can be fixed only approximately. Perhaps 1690 would be as correct a date as it is now possible to fix. The place, therefore, is amongst the very earliest. Built on an H plan, partly of brick and partly of wood, with a large connecting hall, and fine walnut paneling and a particularly richly carved stair, it stands in the first rank. On the land side it is now so masked by trees as not to afford a good picture. We show the water side, the interesting side door of the hall and the great box garden. It was in the little white building across this garden that Thomas Jefferson went to school with the young scion of the house when Peter Jefferson the father of Thomas lived here for a while as executor. The box maze is one of the most perfect and extensive known in this country. In the interior we also show a fireplace wall, and a drawing of the paneling in the great hall, and of the beautiful stair rail and post, (see the two preceeding pages).

Tuckahoe stands for the first important movement in establishing estates west of Richmond. It is still the outstanding place of its age outside of the Tidewater. The house therefore became a social station for travelers of the old families from the Tidewater into the western part of the state. The owner is Mr. Harold Jefferson Coolidge.

Built by Thomas Randolph it passed out from family possession in 1830, but for more than thirty years has been owned by the Coolidges of Boston who come from the Randolph family.

Goochland County is on the north side of the James. The estate stands well up from the river and has numerous accessory edifices. It is a monument of the time of William and Mary when taste had reached its best development and before the rococo of the mid-eighteenth century. It is a matter of congratulation that descendants of these old families are here and there acquiring again the estates which were for a time in other hands. While one may be glad that persons of taste and means, not related to the old families should, when there is no one else to do it, acquire and restore the old places, it is always better not only for reasons of sentiment but from the sounder bases of permanent society, that the owner should be in a line with the builders. No one else can be as interested in an old place and no one else can have as much joy in possessing it as one who can trace his ancestry to the builder.

A RIVER SWIRL

THE JAMES AT SHIRLEY

THE EASTERN SHORE

THE long forefinger reaching down from the Eastern Shore of Maryland for many many miles, pointing toward Norfolk, and forming Chesapeake Bay, and a ramification of inner waters unmatched on the Atlantic coast, is, in spite of its low level surface, a fascinating region. Its flatness is relieved by the endless in and out shore contours, by groups of islands, by the majesty of trees, by a soil teeming throughout like a garden, and by many very ancient estates.

The history is connected with an era antedating the landing of the Pilgrims at Plymouth. Its seclusion and the unwonted agreeableness of its Indian inhabitants, one chief of whom was called the Laugher, permitted its early and peaceful development, and the settling of its people into conservative quiet ways, until one would think he had arrived in a rural English county of the long ago.

Its two counties, Northampton to the south and Accomac on the north, constituting a world apart, are perhaps less exploited than any other old portion of our country. Some day, sweet in anticipation, the author purposes to go there and make a stay long enough to absorb the romance of the history and the full influence of the old architecture. The people know they have something worth knowing and seeing, and they welcome us. At Cape Charles and Accomac as the two headquarters one may find in a few spring days, as we did, enough to enrich one's mind with images of old sail boats, sly pirates, the ghosts of the Custis family, the house-trees of the settlers of three hundred years ago and more.

Among other oddities and artistic stimulations is the debtor's prison at Accomac, happily now standing only for a state of society long past. The utter lack of the use of the human mind in the scheme of legal punishment appears most emphatically in these old jails, in which men in debt were confined, presumably so that they could not work and pay their debts!

Vine Bower near Clifton Forge. High in the hills (page 88) as we come out from Clifton Forge, in a little world apart, is a vine bower, dwelt in by someone who has coaxed nature, never an unwilling assistant, into a partnership of decoration.

An Old Country Road. Away off in the southwest near the crossing of Holston River (page 91) is a scene which the author thinks the finest landscape he found in Virginia. The outlook from the river bridge itself, both up stream and down is good. But an old country road on the east side of the river makes off just before the bridge, skirting an unfolding vision of soft hill outlines, of trees, of a stream accommodatingly turning here and there between the hills. The reader will understand the inevitable foreshortening in a picture, which is sometimes an advantage, but here fails to give the glorious impression that meets the eye.

Roanoke River and City. There are three routes between Roanoke and Salem. That along the river side discloses fine buttonwoods or sycamores, as they are called in Virginia, and other leaning friendly trees like oaks and elms, holding their shady arms above the placid stream (page 92).

The sycamore and oak do for Virginia all and more than all that the maple and elm do for the North.

Roanoke is a revelation to the traveler who has not been in Virginia for some years. The lusty growth of the city, its principal business street being worthy of a metropolis, the picturesque site on the river and its ramifications, are a proof that to these Virginians life is more than meat.

A Lynchburg Memorial (page 116). A monument perhaps unique in America is that grouping at Lynchburg arranged about the stately staircase, from a business street to the higher quarter of the town. A city on a sharp hillside has an asset in such points as these which it would be well to copy from Lynchburg. Seattle might be revolutionized by such treatment of some of its streets, and the same situation will come to the minds of many regarding other cities. Here two churches, a court house and several residences gain a terraced decoration of great merit. At the base, between the double approaches is the monument of the last great war. At the crest is the figure commemorating the war that never should have been had we all loved one another. The broad balustraded landings and the small planted areas are skillfully designed to bring all this distinguished memorial to a focus.

Lynchburg itself with its handsome bridge and beautiful route leading to Natural Bridge has become of late an attractive city.

Not far distant on the Bedford road is the quaint ancient Quaker Memorial Church (page 223). Lynchburg is a convenient center for the inspection of historical and beautiful Virginia, through a range of seventy miles.

In Home From School (page 117) we were happy in meeting several children crossing the brook on a log in the lane. Falling into a chat we naturally answered questions. They lived up the lane; they nodded violent affirmatives when we asked them if they knew where Boston was. As we went on our way we learned that the next village was named Boston, and there the children went to school! This is the lane with so fine a zigzag fence on either side (Virginia Rail Shadows page 231) where the long shadows fall athwart the ribbon road. At the head of that lane one could be satisfied to live and die. Good scenery, good water, good people, good roads, what could one ask more? A few rods beyond we reach a gracious curve of the stream. Flecked by shadows, making soft music, laving the tree roots, Hazel River (Dream River page 245) provides one of the fine compositions of the region.

THE FENCES OF VIRGINIA

WE HAVE referred to the so-called Virginia rail as being the most picturesque of all fences, and greatly to the advantage of the farmer, because it could be easily removed to a new location.

By the side of great estates one often sees solidly built stone walls which probably keep nothing out, and nothing in, but are erected owing to the imitative instinct, following old world fashions. The boulder wall appears very rarely in Virginia as the country does not seem to have been swept in geologic ages by glaciers. In a few mountain sections we see some walls of roughly broken materials. All walls of stone, when preëmpted by vines, double the charm of any road. As one travels from the north there appear in Pennsylvania a multitude of vines, which by the time one reaches Virginia, seize all unoccupied surfaces. That may be said to be one of the most striking characteristics of the South.

The fence formed by a crotch and rail is very rare in Virginia. The post and rail fence such as borders so many Pennsylvania farms, is almost totally lacking. The fence consisting of rails held up between two small posts, connected by withes, is seen occasionally, and when at every connecting post there is a vine the farm borders are very satisfactorily decorated. The grotesque stump fences, seen only in a new country, are scarcely found in Virginia, and we are glad of that. The hurdle fence is seen in a few interior fields on fine estates, especially if there is an English farmer in charge. The board and post fence, not being very durable, and requiring a good deal of lumber, rarely appears.

VIRGINIA BEAUTIFUL

About the dwellings and the gardens the picturesque picket fence appears in a number of our pictures, and adds a good deal to the homelike effect. The new fences being constructed along the state roads are by no means ugly, though it is noticeable that many dangerous points are left unprotected.

The wire fence is inevitably supplanting all others and when vine covered it does not lack attractiveness.

This portion of Virginia has changed less, perhaps, than any other of the thriving parts of the state. The people here work out their own salvation, sending out their produce to the hungry North, and living in the same dwellings inhabited by their fathers for many generations. The advantage to the visitor is that he may lift the curtain on the past. Of course there have been many improvements but they have been along the lines of the past time. It was not necessary for a Virginian to live in a great house to maintain his place in the best society. It was more a matter of family and continuous possession and extent of acreage that gave a man importance. The sense of stability took possession of the minds of planters. They had a tendency to build solidly and beautifully because they anticipated that their grandchildren and all the generations after would inherit from them.

It is interesting to observe how the people of the Tidewater compensated for the lack of hills. They introduced devices in decorations such as were not needed in a hill country, and made up for the lack of a rolling contour by the provision of long garden vistas, by the grouping of great trees, and by the utilization of the banks of streams to provide variety. Even so they could not fully gain all the advantages of an esthetic nature provided by the hill country. Nevertheless, their minds were stimulated, as in Holland, so that they developed more fully on certain lines than did the people in a more naturally beautiful region. Humanity owes most of its discoveries and a great part of its delights from the stress of circumstance and very little to the opulence of materials. That is to say when we are obliged to seek after beauty, or to devise expedients we do so, but not otherwise. Thus what was tame or meager becomes beautiful and rich. Those portions of the world which have the greatest natural advantages are by no means those that are most highly developed esthetically or even otherwise.

A VIRGINIA SWITCHBACK   NATURAL BRIDGE, DOWN STREAM

SOUTHWEST VIRGINIA

PERGOLA STEPS   ROSEHILL ROCK GARDEN

CHELSEA

BACON'S CASTLE FROM THE FRONT

TAPPAHANNOCK CONVERTED JAIL

THE OLD STONE KITCHEN, WINCHESTER

THE PARLOR AT UPPER BRANDON

BACON'S "CASTLE"

WE HAVE not happened to note in Virginia, except in one other instance, the angled chimney stack shown here, but so common in England. It is beautiful, but why so rare, it is hard to comprehend.

The Castle (page 213) which shows here is the old end without the modern chute-like excrescence, and is one of the sturdiest and most fascinating dwellings in Virginia. At the moment it is in serious need of repair, and it is rumored that the title has passed into strong hands, so that we may look forward to seeing the proper thing done. The architecture, unique possibly among early American houses, is highly important, but the fact that there dwelt here a man of virility and vision who led a rebellion against England just a hundred years before the Revolution and a rebellion which came close to success, is a startling chapter in history. Indeed had not Bacon met an untimely death the course of American development might have been radically different. The reader should get the history of Bacon's rebellion, because it is an amazing record. His driving off the royal governor, his burning of Jamestown, thus probably hastening the removal of the capital; his employment of a "navy"; the fire and leadership of the man, which make him a figure of power, all these matters are an epitome of events that came about a century later. But here was a natural, an incipient Napoleon, where leadership had no Fabian quality but drove like lightning to its goal.

The quiet of this retired plantation, after that stormy period, offers a strange contrast. One could love to get away here from the tumult and the shouting and live a recluse.

GUNSTON HALL

IT HAS been previously mentioned that this dwelling is very deceptive from the fact that it looks small, but is really longer than Mount Vernon. The place is very near Pohick church and also very near Mount Vernon being located on the next important point down the river and on the same side. George Mason was a great figure who kept in the background during the Revolution. While he shunned office, his wisdom and learning made him the trusted adviser of Washington and of Jefferson. While Mason's name is

associated with the Bill of Rights, it is known that he was an adviser in the preparation of the Declaration of Independence and in most of the great measures and documents of his time. In a monarchy he would have been called the power behind the throne. His large library, his proximity for consultation with the great leaders of Virginia, and of the North, after the Congress had its seat at Washington, his comprehensive mind and his position as the owner of a great estate, and the lineal descendant of a patriotic English family, all together gave him a prestige such as probably no other Revolutionary patriot enjoyed except such as were in high public office.

Much of the estate has been cut up into small holdings to form residences for Washington people, but the ample grounds and gardens and the old house, lovingly cherished by the present owner, are all a fine background for the noble traditions connected with them.

One wonders what in the course of another generation is to be done regarding these notable old estates. Their history and their beauty of gardens or of merit of architecture, together with the rapidly increasing number of student travelers, who wish to look into what these estates represent, establish a condition such that a private citizen can scarcely enjoy one of these old places, unless he also enjoys keeping open house for all the citizens of the United States.

NOTES ON PICTURES

WE GROW OLD (page 118) pictures a weathered, low roofed old house, under a tree that matches it. In this dwelling all the partitions are beautifully wrought pine sheathing, and at least four doors have wooden latches and latch strings, still in use. There is a recessed porch in front, with a guard rail on the outside. The various rooms open directly on this porch, as well as into one another in a row. A fine old well and windlass by the tree supplies the thirsty passer-by. These people are all smiles, full of human kindness and content.

Ogle Creek (page 127) on the way from Covington to Sulphur Springs, appeals to lovers of trees, mountains and waters; especially the little ledge athwart the current presents a barrier over which the stream tumbles in miniature divided cascades. It is a paradise for a boy at play.

The Mill Canal (page 128) above Sperryville flows above a fairly set farm, where the main stream makes down through the pasture. The region

A FAUQUIER APPROACH

OAKWOOD NEAR WARRENTON

GARDEN COVERED WAYS

HIDE AND SEEK COTTAGE

is replete with attractions. The mill below has its fine spillway, and the stream in the meadow, by morning light is worth returning to see.

Overlooking Roanoke, on a secondary road from the south, a view superb in extent and in blossom time exquisite in color. On a clear day there is a reach across the great southern plain of Virginia. Bowl shaped valleys immediately below, filled with orchards and crossed by the lower gradients of the highway, recommend this spot as a residence superior to anything we saw about Winchester for the picturesqueness of the apple culture. Its nearness to Roanoke also renders it a desirable region. No one should miss this drive, as far at least as the summit of Blue Ridge. (Page 190, An "Airplane" View Above Roanoke.)

The Home Pasture (page 75) is a fair example of the solid houses of the Valley here surrounded by an orchard where the sheep feed—the best combination in this old world; a home, an orchard and a flock! Virginia is one of the states and the last Atlantic state as we go north where sheep still form an important branch of farm life. The flocks are a wholly delightful addition to the aspects of the Valley in particular.

A Blooming Churchyard, at Upperville (page 96) is rare and it is odd that it should be rare, to find apple blossoms in a churchyard. It is a good suggestion which could well be followed up. How seldom do homelike conditions prevail around a church edifice! Yet how appropriate that the house of prayer should be decked with blossoms.

An Alleghany Farm (page 101) brings to mind ancient conditions when the house premises were fenced away from cattle. The custom is not now generally useful but is ornamental, and suggests a cozy aspect. These southwestern farms in Virginia are covered with herds, so that the Biblical phrase could be changed to "the cattle on a myriad hills."

Box Drive, Mt. Bernard (page 102) and a Goochland Estate (page 255) are one plantation. The evenness and the size of these great box trees represent long and careful culture. The extent of the drive is impressive. The estate is on highlands, west of Richmond. Goochland County is peculiar in this, that it is old and yet in parts it is upland. Below Richmond practically all the places on the James and elsewhere are near the sea level. One can, that is, live near Richmond and yet be inland.

Wakefield. The simple single shaft at Wakefield (page 105) erected by the nation in honor of Washington on his supposed birthplace is very satisfactory as to taste. It is a matter of no moment just where he was born. Nothing calamitous will occur if the spot is a mile away.

VIRGINIA BEAUTIFUL

The grove of cedars all along the James on this old estate is admirably clean and sweet. On the immediate shore itself (page 147) the levels are well above the river, while the slope to the strand is covered in spring by a medley of wild flowers. Washington was undoubtedly taken as a babe to play under these trees. The spot is quiet, retired and delightful.

The nation is to build a house on the site of the birthplace. Of course the outlines of the old house are not known, as no pictures exist of it. Yet numerous pictures are extant purporting to show it. The purpose to be served by this erection is difficult to understand, since the old house is gone, and we have the monument. So rapid is the growth of tradition that it will not be a generation before the great mass of the public will not merely suppose the new house to be exactly like the old, but even to be a "restoration." The project, therefore, will simply be the means of giving a wrong impression, even though that is not the intention.

The plan calls for an attractive, simple, conventional house, of the sort so often seen yet in Virginia, of one story with a row of dormer windows and end chimneys. The location of Wakefield is such that only one person visits it to thousands who visit Mt. Vernon. Its retired situation, in Westmoreland County, the Northern Neck, will always leave it comparatively unmolested by crowds. But its proximity to Stratford and Mt. Airy, all in short driving distance from Fredericksburg, should ensure a journey to this point on the part of anyone who wishes to see the best of Virginia.

Montpelier. This imposing place has been extended since the days when it was the home of Madison. The lands however have naturally diminished. The estate is a good example of the English conditions, under which landed property received recognition. Many thousands of acres under one ownership, in this fine county of Orange, naturally acquired representation, through its owner, in the political scheme. James Madison, Sr., was what in England would have been called a member of the county families.

The future president, his son, marrying the tactful and accomplished widow, Dorothea Payne Todd, entertained with her help on his superb hill outlook. Dolly Madison became, socially and politically, a power in the state and nation and her popularity was of great assistance to her husband.

While Montpelier Mansion is not open to the public the author was accorded the courtesy of obtaining many pictures here, of one of the largest, most formal terraced gardens in Virginia. A stream passing through the grounds at one side forms a small lake, which with its surrounding trees is an object of beauty (page 111). Near by is the garden temple (page 171) perfectly set as an accessory decoration, at the proper distance from the great house. The size of the house itself exceeds that of any other that came under observation. It is so large in fact that the mass seen at a distance without anything about to give scale is deceptively underrated (page 14).

The Terrace of Steps (page 76) with a massed box and other foliage is one of the central points in the garden. While Montpelier Terraces (page 198) has been chosen to illustrate in part the amphitheatre, or horseshoe, any one of several points might equally well be chosen to vary the outlook. A Garden of Rose Trees (page 60) like most garden pictures, is never a fair representation of the gorgeous coloring and multiplied fragrance. Across the Boxwood (page 61) is a somewhat better impression, while a Montpelier Arbor (page 88) may serve as one of many gracious arches such as abound on the borders.

Orange County where Montpelier is forms an extension of a country similar to Albemarle, the heart of the Piedmont.

Maxwell is a dwelling and a garden growing beautiful under the care of the McVeighs. The Flounces of Dorothy Perkins (page 132) is one of the almost natural decorations. Within moderate distance of Charlottesville, this and other foci of interest are available in garden week.

Morven near Charlottesville. As there is another Morven in Virginia we designate this one as above. There is a pleasure to be derived from illustrating this place, because there are so many standpoints affording winning prospects. In Morven Drive (page 133) appears the way between the ell of the residence and a smaller house on the right. From the Garden (page 153) one looks back toward the ell of the residence.

The Morven Kitchen (page 76) shows the generous provision of a great fireplace and a separate oven for the old time cooking.

In the Cottage Row (page 240) the first building is the exterior of that kitchen, the lane leading away past garden and quarters. The Old Door (page 97) of a service building shows the hole for the latch string, a quaint wooden latch and old hardware.

Within the residence the object that gets first attention is the beautiful mantel secured in France by Thomas Jefferson for his friend, the owner of the house. It belongs to the period near the close of the eighteenth century when excellent taste prevailed.

This estate is kept in perfect condition by the Charles A. Stones, the garden also affording us for this volume other illustrations.

Seven Oaks. This estate is so called by the Harrises, the owners, from the magnificent oaks named after seven presidents. Going to this place absolute strangers we were received with every consideration, and allowed also to obtain pictures of certain pieces of rare furniture. The garden is laid out in a skillful color scheme and the pergola is artistic to a degree.

The front (page 149) is equally good from the garden side. It is shown from this side because the old well canopy is so fine a scheme of decoration.

Quarters are shown (page 44) well bowered with vines. The estate is not distant from Charlottesville, and though it is not listed among the large roster of attractions we found it better worth while than many places widely known.

The Keim House. An old residence whose woodwork and furniture are important, and in combination very important is found on a quiet street of Fredericksburg in a location still agreeable. The hall, although it is not illustrated, is good. The drawing room has on each side of the fireplace a long elliptical arch, with recesses beneath. The decorative scheme reminds one somewhat of the Royal House in Medford, Massachusetts. The fully detailed and gracefully designed cornice, overmantel, mantel, and pilasters are very beautiful, the more so as they are flanked by Sheraton chairs of a pattern that has appealed to the more exacting tastes.

On the opposite side of the room the main door into the hall (page 44) shows a broken pediment decoration, a well paneled door, with ancient brass box lock and drop handle, and on the left a good transition chair. The library overmantel (page 65) displays an odd and pleasing design, rare in some of its details. The dining room is interesting. The courtesy shown by the owner was most thoughtful.

Claremont. This celebrated old place, which claims a relation to Thackeray's Virginians, has some features unique and others unusual. The approach on the land side (page 157) shows a rarely attractive, small white house, one of the accessory buildings, which by humorous hyperbole is called, and truthfully, "the smallest five story house." A little window in the very peak, hidden by foliage, must be included in the count. The overworked and inaccurate adjective cunning (which means cute?) is the only one that comes to mind for the description. The setting of this house, and its restored connection with the entrance to the residence, all brooded over by the grace of fine trees, is altogether distractingly lovely. A low garden border (page 197) with a turf walk leading down through the orchard to the river

THE OLD QUAKER CHURCH, AMHERST-BEDFORD

THE LITTLE HOUSE BY THE ROAD

WESTOVER LAWN

BYRD MONUMENT LANE, WESTOVER

A HOT SPRINGS CURVE

ROSEHILL BORDERS

UNDER THE APPALACHIANS

THE LONG DOWN GRADE

forms one side of the lawn. The rambling dwelling shows several aspects of roof line that give an unusual liveliness to the house. There is a bit of the garden at one end which suggests a patio.

One of the chambers has been slept in by so many presidents and other distinguished personages that time would fail one to name them all. Just think of all before the war of 1861, in office or out, and you will not require to erase many names from your list.

Brigadier General Cocke and his wife are the present fortunate owners. The Cocke name was connected with the house from of old. The residence stands on a very gentle knoll from which a terrace drops to the main level, at a good elevation above the river. A curious paved ramp leads down the terrace, whether to take the place of steps or to accommodate a wheel chair one wonders (page 30).

All in all the house piques one's curiosity. A basement has been admirably fitted with simple early furniture. A great hall or assembly room connects the driveway end with the garden side of the house.

The date of this plantation is well back in the seventeenth century.

A Little Mountain Valley. In the horseshoe curves of the highway over Temple Mountain are enclosed some delectable nooks dear to the lover of little fields, minor glens, pasture slopes, natural terraces and the spring fashions on trees. The locust ornaments the mountain grades.

When vines and blossoms also claim the support of a tree we are certainly called upon to take notice as on page 140. Here for miles is a domain of fancy, a landscape for a poet. Why do the poets live in unlovely places? If they need a stimulus to the imagination they could find it.

Temple Mountain by either ascent and along the summit stands high among Virginia's best scenery.

About St. Paul also (pages 147 and 172) Pennington Gap, Stone Gap, all in the toe of Virginia, she could put the many children that have nowhere else to go and do well by them. Why, there is room in upland Virginia for fifty, nay a hundred where one lives poorly now. There are not lacking abundant sources of natural wealth, to crown it there is crest on crest, valley on valley, curve on curve, a grace and glory, a witchery of flowers and foliage, a sky where the white fleeced flocks move gently and hide or reveal the deep azure beyond.

Virginia is at the portal of a future which expands fanlike, spreading like the dawn of a grander day. When all her people are open to the appealing of the past, as they may be, when all of them by a nobler system of education grasp, as so many have done, the heritage of the ages, who will set a limit to what Virginia may show in a hundred years, where beauty may reign over the home, the thought, the works of all her people.

ARLINGTON

IT IS a strange coincidence that this house where General Lee lived should face Washington. The architectural lines follow those of a Greek temple and are very imposing in their situation. Perhaps this is the only house in Virginia which stands for three very distinct interests. In the first place the residence was built by George Washington Parke Custis, who had been brought up as Washington's son, but was the grandson of Martha Washington. He built here early in the nineteenth century.

Then he married into the Lee family and his wife was Mary, daughter of William Fitzhugh Lee of Chatham; this couple's daughter married Robert E. Lee. She also inherited Arlington where they lived until 1861.

In the third place when the estate was taken by the National government it became the center of the great cemetery for soldiers. Now officers only are buried here, but formerly the rank and file also had here their last resting place. Here the author's father is buried.

The house therefore stands for the Custises and Washington. It stands for the Lee family. It stands for the memory of the soldier dead. These three very striking salients of interest together with its impressive situation bring it to the attention of every visitor to Washington, even to those who do not go to Mt. Vernon.

We may say that the World War cemented the North and the South since all fought together on the battlefield of the world. This war also followed another war in which the whole country was concerned for the liberation of Cuba. Arlington therefore stands for three wars the second and the third of which united those who had been opposed in 1861. There are then here the graves of the Custises and therefore of the mother of General Lee, and the graves of many patriots whose names were not mentioned in history and the graves of a great corps of notable men who have led the armies of their reunited country. In many particulars it is the most important and sacred ground not only in Virginia but in the whole nation. Many hearts throb here and many eyes drop tears.

WILLIAMSBURG AS IT USED TO BE

AN AMUSING detail in the building of Williamsburg is the fact that it was laid out on paper without reference to the contour of the site. As a consequence it was found that the Duke of Gloucester Street would run into a glen. The direction of the street therefore was changed so that the main central edifice from which it started is not on a true axis with the street.

Another noticeable feature is that while all the college buildings and all the edifices erected by the state for its own use are of brick, nearly all, however, if not all, of the private houses were of wood. Also it would be noted that by far the greater number are humble in size. It is to be inferred that even the rich planters of Virginia who built homes for the "season" in Williamsburg did not think it worth while to duplicate in dignity or size or material the mansions on their estates. Indeed it was a somewhat magnificent gesture to erect residences of any character for the brief term during which the House of Burgesses sat. The procedure followed of course indicates that families of high social position came with household servants, and bag and baggage, to take advantage of the social features offered. Whereas the modern day might be content with hotels, the habit of entertaining in a private house, so entrenched in the popular mind in England and in plantation life here, induced a more general separate provision for the First Families of Virginia, even when, as at Williamsburg, those families were away from home.

Thus we see that even the famous Raleigh Tavern was a wooden structure. The small middle class or any professional person without a landed estate who perhaps resided the year around at Williamsburg, needed a residence. Such, however, was the excellent taste of the period that not even the miniature dwellings of two rooms (beside which of course there was always an out building for a kitchen and servant) lacked pleasing and harmonious architectural detail, and was as perfect in its way as the great house. Indeed we have never been able fully to have determined why the little house appeals to the imagination more than the great house. Thus we see that a French queen tiring of the magnificence of her palaces erected a little cottage in her gardens and for some reason or other it was there that her heart was. Why even persons of wealth consciously or unconsciously admire the little house is something one has always desired to see explained satisfactorily.

VIRGINIA RAIL SHADOWS

SPRING LANE

We, all of us, are drawn toward what we have named cozy. Whatever the psychology behind the architecture we are indebted to Williamsburg for what we may call a series of all grades of domiciles from the minute to the magnificent, the latter of course being the residence of the governor.

On page 15, the description of the copperplate on pages 16 and 17, does not enter into the illustrations at the bottom of those pages. Whether it was thought that the illustration of the beetle and the spider would attract immigrants we do not know. The tobacco plant, however, would seem to have had its attractions. The comely Indian mother, her hair neatly done in a Grecian coil, and her papoose, dressed for summer weather, are certainly important and are properly scaled very much larger than her lord and master, who is a very insignificant figure in the opposite corner. She is pointing for the child at the beetle which is large enough to devour the infant who nevertheless views the horrendous creature with true Spartan placidity.

We have been very happy in making an enlarged and clarified plate from the photograph furnished us. The discovery of the original plate, an amazing find in itself, becomes the more important since all the edifices here illustrated on the second or central panel are to be faithfully erected in the restoration work. It is noticeable that the subordinate buildings in No. 6 are precisely the same thing as some of the cottages of which we have been speaking above.

We take occasion here to mention the truly wonderful quality of the mason's work in the dwellings of Virginia. Some of this work nearly three hundred years old seems as perfect today as when it was erected. Some of it seems to bear no evidence of having been pointed. The perfect courses are in a precisely smooth plane. Why these masons were possessed of such an almost uncanny skill apparent in nearly all the Virginia work surpasses one's comprehension. The inevitable conclusion is forced upon us, that, both in architecture and in furniture the time of Queen Anne far surpassed anything that has followed it.

Kenmore

Kenmore, one would say, is destined to be the fourth place in importance in Virginia, but the third in frequence of visitation. The energy and optimism of the secretary of the society, in whose possession it is, are working wonders in the way of restorations and decorations. To accommodate space

the four spandrels of the highly decorated ceiling in the room at the left of
the garden entrance, are shown on pages 95, 96, 97, and 98. They represent the four seasons. For the spring, the palm; for the summer, the
grape; for the autumn, the oak; and for the winter, the mistletoe. These
motives are similar to others at Mt. Vernon, and it is thought that they were
suggested by Washington to his sister Betty. This was the home of Col.
Lewis, the brother-in-law and close friend of Washington. It has not only
noble associations, owing to the unselfish character of the man who built it,
and to Betty Washington, who was always on such terms of affectionate intimacy with her brother, but also because the house itself is a handsome rep-
resentative of its time. It has restored accessory buildings and occupies a
wonderful site being kept in its original space without encroachment of other
structures. The mantels and overmantels are especially good. The mantels are carved as seen on pages 29 and 163. It has been a puzzle to know
whether the mantel was painted white to match the overmantel which is in
plaster. The most striking of them all, however, is on page 241, and represents the celebrated fable showing the house, the castle and the church,
as the exponents of three orders of human society. All this work, together
with the fine ceiling, has been wonderfully preserved, when one considers
that this house was in the swirling track of the war. It is said that Washington assisted in arranging for this excellent decoration.

All the rooms in this house, including the hall, are interesting, and are
being restored even to the original tinting of the walls, as precisely as possible. Since Fredericksburg is near Washington, and on the direct route north
and south, it is likely to be visited more and more, especially as there are
many other places in town highly worthy of attention. Near at hand is the
home for thirteen years, the western years of her life, of Mary the mother of
Washington. He desired to have her free from the cares of a country home
and it was, of course, quite delightful to be so near Kenmore where her
daughter was, and where she was often a guest. It is hinted that she would
have been glad to go to Mt. Vernon, but that Washington was wise enough
to advise her that she would not be as happy there and would be worn out by
the continual visitation. It may be so, and also it may be that the old wise
scheme of what was equivalent to a dower house for the mother of the owner
of a place was thought better. However good and noble she and Martha
Washington were, they probably needed two houses. Neither the exterior
nor the interior of her cozy quarters are much to look at, but they were very
ample for a family of one. Her parlor is shown on page 41, and indicates

HILLS ON HOLSTON RIVER

BULL RUN BANKS, PRINCE WILLIAM COUNTY

THE HILL PASTURES NEAR LEBANON

DOGWOOD, NATURAL FOREST

rather late work for her period. It might have been done during the last years of her life. The room in which she died and the fireplace at which she sat is the older room of the house. It is bright and pleasant and on the first floor. It was here that Washington saw her in the later days, and it is here that he is represented as kneeling by her side, and receiving her blessing (page 87). The garden is small but doubtless afforded her, who loved a garden, ample recreation.

There must be twenty or thirty places in Fredericksburg that ought to be visited. A delightful spot is the Quarters, page 96, which has another and longer approach (page 23). It is very surprising that a place so fiercely fought over should have so many good old homes and so much fine furniture as Fredericksburg.

Here are also the monuments of Mary Washington, very satisfactory in its simplicity, and of Washington's chief of the medical staff of the army, and intimate friend.

Rosehill. The home of the head of the society which has Stratford in its keeping, Mrs. Massie, is beautifully located near Charlottesville. The gardens are laid out in a modern fashion, very successfully, and it is a pleasure to delineate so many scenes within them, on page 35, where the charming light motives of pale roses and light flowering borders are emphasized, and on page 43, which is very gorgeous in its coloring. The shrubbery is happily disposed with the taller trees to form fascinating walks with many surprising curves. These appear again on page 124. There is a charming little rock and water garden too intimate for large effects on page 210. Finally Rosehill Borders (page 225) is a delightful prospect.

Stratton

The drawing on the following page represents Stratton, an Accomac County plantation house. It is more pleasing than some others owing to the grouping of the dwelling with a great barn. To descriptions elsewhere in this volume we may add an allusion to the totally opposite tendences of the Nordic and the Latin races, regarding residences. The Latins everywhere love to group their residences and towns. The spirit of the Nordic peoples was to dwell in the midst of one's acres. It is a searching question to ask whether this independence and strength of character is dying away. Our ancestors seemed to have no fear of isolation. They went to the middle of their plantations and there erected their dwellings. It was the better way. It encouraged individuality.

238

AN ORCHARD COTTAGE

WYCO RIVER

FARMINGTON, CHARLOTTESVILLE

COTTAGE ROW, MORVEN

A BEAUTIFUL OLD CHURCH

THE FABLE MANTEL, KENMORE

FROM THE PASTURE RAMPARTS

The Picturesque in Transportation

The canal boat (page 190) was perhaps the most picturesque method of transportation. It is difficult in this generation to understand the immense and universal interest in canals in the early part of the nineteenth century. There was scarcely an inland village on a brook which did not see itself as a mart for world products through the canal boat, which it is believed would be made available almost everywhere. We note that a prominent New York state official has recently stated that transportation by canal boat across New York is the most interesting recreation a traveler can enjoy. While the canals were strictly utilitarian they could not escape being openings to much superb scenery.

The railway which follows in the next period is probably the least satisfactory method of traveling so far as seeing the country is concerned. It notoriously goes in at the back doors of all cities. The speed of its trains cannot be regulated to the convenience of the traveler. It does not come to a pause with its trains at the best points for observation.

The modern highway from the very fact that its curves required good engineering, is picturesque. As this method of traveling is likely to be the usual one at least for moderate distances, it becomes the duty of the state to guard whatever esthetic features a highway naturally possesses, and to foster the development of beauty on the borders of the highway. The eventual total abolition of poles with wiring is the goal to seek after. Such encumbrances are unsightly and dangerous and communication is liable to interruption by storm so as to cripple the system at the very time when disasters may make it most important. The companies which are filling the roads with their wires should be assisted in all reasonable ways in adopting the underground transmission, and on all main roads, such transmission should be insisted upon.

The next matter of attention is the bare borders of the road, where cuts or fills occur. In some states, as in Connecticut, this matter is being especially cared for by a landscaping department, so as to do away with all the bare gravel slopes. It is probable that the saving effected in the preventing of wash by storms will be enough to offset the expense of planting. The railroads have often found it to their advantage to foster growths along such places.

In another connection I have mentioned the importance of providing, here and there, outlooks by the side of the highway at important viewpoints.

In most cases it is at these very points where bushes or some dense growth interferes with the view. These are not unimportant matters, although persons in charge of our roads are slow in seeing them. Obviously it is to the advantage of any district that travelers should visit it and be kept in it as long as possible, whether as summer guests or as investors. There is nothing that brings such large dividends as that which is expended in covering the scars of a countryside. If a region gets a reputation for being beautiful, the real estate multiplies in value. We are talking on this low financial plane because that is the aspect of the case which most interests the taxpayer. If we make it easy to reach a destination and then make that destination attractive we have helped ourselves and helped our neighbors, and made life better.

These movements are slow in starting just as the good roads are a matter of less than a generation. Nevertheless the wealth and intelligence of the country is sufficient, once it is enlisted, to work a rapid change in the way of rendering our countrysides beautiful. For instance, it is becoming more and more dangerous and in some cases even against the law, to park a car on a country highway. There is always an opening where a small space may be graveled to afford a stopping place. On some of the most superb roads in this country that small attention has not been paid to the public. We have found that at Richmond, at the Historical Society rooms and the Chamber of Commerce, there is a good deal of information as to the location of beautiful old places. There is not, however, anywhere, any sort of information as to where the beautiful scenery in Virginia is to be found. Garage men almost never know anything of this matter, nor of the condition of roads even. That can be ascertained by a monthly map issued by the enterprise of the State Highway Commission. It should be easily feasible to list the beautiful or interesting points in every neighborhood, and to provide a small pamphlet to be found in every sizable town which should contain this information. When one gets away from the center there is always in every state a lamentable lack of knowledge of the things worth seeing. Hotels in particular will find it to their interest to have a careful list of all such points with a word or two mentioning their peculiar merits. Some hotels are alert to the importance of this matter. They understand that it may hold their guests with them for a considerable number of days and not merely over night.

Even the best prepared of these lists, however, show that they have been done in a haphazard manner, not above a half of the places of interest being mentioned even in the best outlines. There ought to be at least about

DREAM RIVER

A LOUISA COUNTY CREEK

A GARDEN BORDER AND ARBOR

twenty points in Virginia, around which should be grouped, in a list, whatever may appeal to the traveler in a circuit of forty miles. Information of this sort is very difficult to get at in any state. It is a pleasure to say that more attention has been paid to this matter in Virginia than elsewhere. But we have often found that a very beautiful old place or magnificent piece of road is entirely overlooked in such lists as exist. If the trouble is to be taken to make such lists at all the additional trouble and expense of making them fuller would be very small. All local historical societies could naturally and would cheerfully, one would say, take on this matter of opening their country to the traveler. The date, material, name, extent, and location of an interesting old place may all be told in a very few lines. The historical societies may not consider themselves also as arbiters of what is beautiful in their landscapes, but there is no reason why they should not so consider themselves. The Chambers of Commerce are trying to guide the public to some degree, but it needs the persons of learning and taste in a town to mention briefly the points now available by the new roads that are worth finding out.

Of course guide books are the natural places for such information. But there are no guide books of this sort, such as abound in Europe. Even if such works existed the information they contain requires a good deal of attention and no wise man wishes to have his nose in a guide book while he is passing beautiful scenery or historic monuments. Something briefer and simpler is required. The state highway markers are excellent in this regard but they do not extend to esthetic matters and they are not located, as a rule, where they may be read. Of course the American is supposed to have reached such a degree of keenness that he who runs may read. It is a false assumption.

Besides, these markers do not help one to arrange a tour. They are accidentally discovered as one travels, and they are very good provided only there were just space to pull one side where they are located. The garden book is excellent, but it directs us to many places where the gardens are meager, and omits many wonderful old houses where there may not be any garden. Further, if touring in Virginia is to be confined to a week or two the public and the people of Virginia are destined to be disappointed. People must go when they can, and the highways are always open. The old churches and court houses and most notable historic points can be seen at any season of the year. Kindly Virginians, help us along! If you have lovely scenery, make it easy to find it. Not every man can spend months in ferreting out the hidden beauties of the countryside. We know from trying experience that one often goes within a few rods of an important or beautiful object and learns incidentally long afterwards that he has passed it unwittingly because of the very lack of available information. This book is written partly with the idea of calling attention to such places. We believe that many of the old houses and good landscapes that are shown here have not been previously available. Nevertheless this is not a guide book. It is more something to be read or enjoyed pictorially before or after a journey. Obviously it cannot mention more than one point in ten that is worth mentioning.

INTERESTING VISITATION POINTS

POINTS preceded by a star are generally open to the public. Some other places are scarcely accessible except through acquaintance or important introductory letters. The list is given by counties.

Accomac County, Eastern Shore

Bowman's Folly, Custis Place, Deep Creek, Margaret Academy, Melvin, Mount Custis, Mount Wharton, Roseland, Shepherd's Plain, St. George's Church, Stratton, Twin Houses (many), Welbourne, Horntown.

Flat, with low islands.

Albemarle County, about Charlottesville

*Ash Lawn, Belmont, Belvoir, Birdwood, Carlton, Castle Hill, Cismont, Cloverfield, Edge Hill, Enniscorthy, Estouteville, *Farmington, Gale Hill, Hopedale, Kinlock, Lego, Maxfield, Mirador, *Monticello, Monticola, Morven, Mountain Top, Pantop, Plain Dealing, Redlands, Ridgeway, Rosehill, Rougment, Shadwell, Sunnyside, Tallwood, Woodville, *University of Virginia.

Hilly, beautiful with streams, and woodland.

Alexandria County, near Washington

*Arlington, *Carlisle House, *Christ's Church, Gadsby's Tavern, Memorial Masonic Monument.

Hills, rolling country, streams, and Potomac River.

VIRGINIA BEAUTIFUL

Alleghany County, Western, Beyond the Valley

Falling Spring Cascade, Falling Spring Stream.
Mountains, streams, scenic roads.

Appomattox, Western Central

Apple Blossoms, Place of surrender.
Rolling or level.

Augusta County, Head of Shenandoah Valley (Staunton)

Apple Blossoms, Folly, Natural Chimneys, Shenandoah Natural Forest, Old Stone Church, Stuart House, Wilson Birthplace.
Rolling country, mountains on each side.

Bath County, west of Shenandoah

Boxwood Farm, Gramercy Farm, Green Valley, Hobby Horse Farm, Hot Springs, Montcalm, Roseloe, Three Hills, Warm Springs, Wallawhaloola, The Yard.
Mountainous, beautiful.

Bedford County, near Lynchburg

Gorge of the James, Ivy Cliff, Poplar Forest, Otter Burn.
Scenic roads and streams.

Botetourt County, west of Natural Bridge

Eagle Rock Park, Peaks of Otter.
Streams, mountains, forests.

Brunswick County, southern tier, southwest of Petersburg

Fort Christiana, Millville Plantations, The Woodlands.
Slightly rolling, open country.

Buckingham County, central Virginia

Bellmont.
Level or slightly rolling.

Campbell County, south of Lynchburg

Green Hill, James River and Bridge, Lynchburg, Quaker Memorial Church, Red Hill, Staunton Hill, Sweetbrier.
Rolling and mountainous.

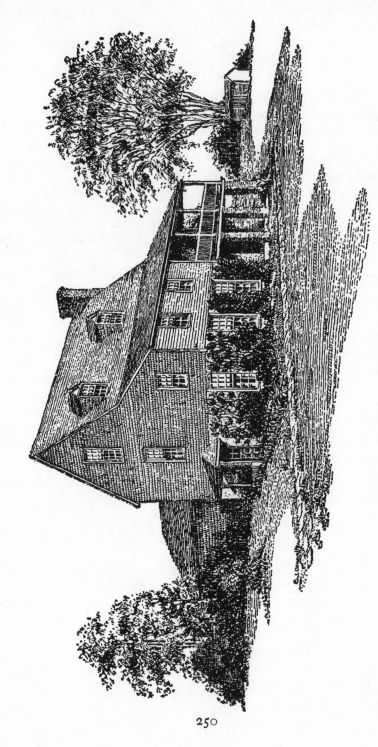

THE ORDINARY GLOUCESTER

Caroline County, south of Fredericksburg

Fairfield Place, Place of Stonewall Jackson's death, Ormesby.
Rolling country.

Charles City County, southeast of Richmond

Berkeley, Hampstead, River Edge, Sherwood Forest, Shirley, Teddington, Wayanoke, Westover.

Charlotte County, southern central

Greenfield, Ingleside, Mulberry Hill, Red Hill, Roanoke (residence).
Level or rolling.

Chesterfield County, southwest of Richmond

Ampthill, Black Heath (Chesterfield), Courthouse, Eppington, Falling
Creek Mill, Salsbury.
Level or rolling.

Clarke County, east of Winchester

Audley, Annfield, Carter's Hall, Clifton, Fairfield, Long Branch, Miss
Rose MacDonald's (Berryville), Pagebrook, Saratoga, The Shenandoah,
Tuyleries.
Hilly and rolling. Fine streams and trees.

Craig County, western

Craig Healing Springs, Virginia Mineral Springs.
Mountainous, wild, beautiful.

Culpepper County, northwest of Fredericksburg

Betty Washington Lewis Tomb, Culpepper (an interesting village).
Level or beautiful rolling country.

Cumberland County, central Virginia

Clifton, Effingham Tavern, Oakland, Union Hall.
Level or rolling country.

Dinwiddie County, Petersburg and south

Appomattox Manor, Battlefields, Battersea, Blandford Church, Bollingbroke, Center Hill, Mansfield, Violet Bank.
Level or rolling.

Elizabeth City County, Newport News and north

Fortress Monroe, Hampton Institute, St. John's Church (Hampton).
Level.

Essex County, on the south bank of the Rappahannock

Blandford, Gaymount, Tappahannock Village and Jail, Vauters
Church.

Fairfax County, southwest of Washington

Bannister, Bellevue, Berry Hall, *Courthouse, Great Falls of the Potomac, Gunston Hall, *Mount Vernon, *Pohick Church, Rippon, Wellington.
Rolling and hilly, fine trees.

Fauquier County, rolling and hilly

Clovelly, Gordonsdale, Montebello, North Wales, Oakhall (Marshall
Place), Oakwood, Rockhill.

Fluvanna County, southeast of Charlottesville

Lower Bremo, Point of Fork.
Level or rolling.

Frederick County, Winchester and vicinity

Abraham's Delight, Hite House (9 miles south), General Morgan House,
Old Stone Kitchen, Springdale, Vaucluse, Washington Headquarters, Wil-
low Lawn.
Rolling country.

Gloucester County, north of Yorktown

Abington Church, Airville, Belleville, *Botetourt Tavern, Carter's
Creek or Fairfield, Durham Massie, Ehrington Farm, The Exchange, North
River, Goshen, Hesse, Powhatan's Chimney (fallen), Rosewell, Sherwood,
The Ordinary, Timberneck, Toddsbury (3), Ware Church, Warner Hall,
Whitehall (Ware River), Whitemarsh.
Level, good trees, fine shores.

Goochland County, west of Richmond

Bolling Hall, Dover, Howards Neck, Mt. Bernard, Rock Castle, Sabot
Hill, Tuckahoe.
Rolling or level.

Grayson County, southwest

Buck Mountain (4680 feet).
Beautiful mountain scenery.

Halifax County, on southern line, Roanoke River

Dan River, Halifax Village, Mildendo, Staunton Hill.
Level and rolling.

Hanover County, north of Richmond

Cloverlea, Court House, Edgewood, Fork Church, Hickory Hill, Newmarket, Oakland.
Level or rolling.

Henrico County, Richmond

Adams House, Agecroft Hall, Allen House, Anderson House, Archer House, Bremo (barn), Brookhill, Bullock House, Capitol, Crump House, Gamble House, Governor's Mansion, Gray House, Malvern Hill, Marshall House, McChane House, Monumental Church; Reveille, The Oaks, Powhatan (near Richmond), St. John's Church, Swan Tavern, Valentine Museum, Virginia House, Westmoreland Club, White House of Confederacy, Wilton (near Richmond).

Isle of Wight, east of Norfolk

*St. Luke's Church, 1632.

James City County, Williamsburg

Ambler, *Ancient College Hall, *Ancient Jail, Ancient Mulberry Trees (Williamsburg), *Bruton Church (Williamsburg), Blair House, Carter's Grove (Connections new), Carter House, Coleman House, *Courthouse, *Jamestown Church, Many Houses (restored), Memorial of First Communion (Jamestown), National Monument (Jamestown); *Old Powder Horn, Page House, Pocahontas Monument (Jamestown), Porto Bello (near), *Raleigh Tavern, Relic House (Jamestown), Saunders House, Statue, Lord Botetourt, Tazewell House, Tucker House, Well of Death (Jamestown); *William & Mary College, *Wythe House.

King and Queen County, north of Westpoint

Mattapony Church.
Level, and with good streams and trees.

King George County, east of Fredericksburg
Cleve, Lamb's Creek Church.
Level, attractive shores and trees.

King William County, northeast of Richmond
Chelsea, on the Mattapony, King William Courthouse, Elsing Green, Horn Quarter.
Level.

Lancaster County, southern end of Northern Neck
Christ's Church, Epping Forest, Laurel Roadsides, St. Mary's White Chapel, Towle's Point.
Rolling or level.

Lee County, extreme southwest
Cumberland Gap, Pennington Gap, Scenic Roads, Fine Forests.

Loudoun County, northwest of Washington
Foxcroft, Malvern Park, Methodist Church in Leesburg, Oak Hill (Monroe's Place); Oaklands (near Leesburg), The Potomac River, Raspberry Plain (near Leesburg).
Rolling country, well wooded.

Louisa County, east of Charlottesville
Bracket's, Iona, Sylvania, Westend.
Level, slightly rolling.

Madison County, northwest of Orange
Projected Shenandoah National Park, Woodberry Forest.

Mathews County, east end of Middle Neck
Auburn, Green Plains, Poplar Grove, Tide Mill, Wind Mill.
Level or rolling, interesting bays.

Macklenburg County, southern line, central
Prestwold.
Level or rolling.

Middlesex County, south of Rappahannock, at mouth
Rosegill.
Level, good trees and shores.

Montgomery County, southwest

Springfield House.

Mountainous, fine streams and forests, scenic roads.

Nansemond County, southeast

Suffolk, Old Port.

Level.

Nelson County, southwest of Charlottesville

Edgewood, Liberty Hall, Oakridge, Soldier's Joy, Union Hill.

Rolling and hilly.

New Kent County, east of Richmond

Cedar Grove, Eltham, Hampstead, Providence Forge, St. Peter's Church.

Level.

Norfolk County

Holly Lodge, Old Colonial House, Old Donation House, Lawson Hill, Myer House, St. Paul's Church, Talbert Hall.

Level.

Northampton County, eastern shore

Brownville, Cessford, Dickenson, Hungar's Church, Vaucleuse, West House (Deep Creek).

Level, good trees and winding shores.

Northumberland County, Northern Neck

Ditchley, Mantua, Springfield.

Good trees, broken shores and inlets, level.

Orange County, northeast of Charlottesville

Barbersville, Frascali, Germanna, Horsehoe, Montepelier, Peliso, Rocklands, St. Thomas Church.

Rolling, beautiful.

Page County, off the Shenandoah near New Market

*Endless Caverns, Egypt House, *Luray Caveins.

Mountainous or rolling.

Pittsylvania County, Danville

Berry Hill, City Library (Danville, last capital of Confederacy), Chatham Hall, Eldon, Dogwood Blossoms (easterly), Gilbert Place, Mountainview.
Rolling country.

Powhatan County, west of Richmond

Beaumont, Bellmead, Norwood, Paxton.
Level or rolling.

Prince Edward County

Clover Forest.

Prince George County, east of Petersburg

Appomattox Manor, Brandon, Flower de Hundred, Merchant's Hope Church, Upper Brandon.
Level or rolling, good trees.

Princess Anne County

Cape Henry, Eastern Shore Chapel, Helleston, Old Lynnhaven, Sand Dunes, Thoroughgood House (about 1635).
Flat, with interesting estuaries.

Prince William County, southwest of Mt. Vernon

Bull Run, Bull Run Bridge, Falls of Occoquan.
Rolling.

Rappahannock County, east of Luray Caverns

Sperryville, attractive stream and mill.
Rolling and hilly.

Richmond County, east of Rappahannock, Northern Neck

Bladensfield, Farnham Church (restored), Laurel Banks, Menokui, Mount Airy, Sabine Hall.
Level or rolling.

Roanoke County, southwest

Buena Vista, *Crystal Springs, *Dixie Caverns, Greenfield, Hollins, Fotheringay, Lone Oak, Fort Lewis, Monterey, Roanoke River.
Attractive river, low mountains, good trees.

Rockbridge County, *Natural Bridge*

Birthplace of Sam Houston, Goshen Pass, *Natural Bridge, Lexington and environs, *Virginia Military Institute, *Washington and Lee University, With the Tomb of Lee.
Beautiful natural scenery.

Rockingham County, *Shenandoah Valley*

*Blue Grottoes, *Grand Caverns, Intermittent Spring, Lincoln Homestead, *Massanutten Caverns, Mole Hill, Shenandoah National Forest.
Rolling or mountainous, attractive.

Russell County, *southwest*

Clinch River, Fine Mountain Scenery, Scenic Roads.

Scott County, *southwest*

Clinch River, Natural Tunnel, Scenic Roads, Mountains.

Shenandoah County, *northwest*

Apple Blossoms, Bushand House, Seven Bends of the Shenandoah, *Shenandoah Caverns, Shenandoah River (north fork), Woodstock Village.

Smyth County, *southwest*

General William Campbell's Home and Tomb, Fine Mountains, Scenic Roads.

Spottsylvania County, *south of Fredericksburg*

See under Stafford County

Stafford County (*Fredericksburg*)

*Aquia Church, Boscobel, Chatham, Fall Hill, Federal Hill, Keim House (Fredericksburg), *Kenmore (Fredericksburg), Marye House (Fredericksburg), Hugh Mercer's Shop, Hugh Mercer's Monument, *Monroe's Law Office, Spring Dale, Rising Sun Tavern, *Mary Washington's House, Mary Washington's Monument, Roxbury.
Rolling or hilly.

Surry County, *east of Petersburg*

Bacon's Castle, Claremont, Four Mile Tree, Warren or Rolfe House.
Level or rolling.

Washington County, southwest

Old Byars House, Fork of Holston River, Grave of William King, The Meadows.

Beautiful river and mountain scenery.

Westmoreland County, Northern Neck

Kirnan, Stratford (The Lee Homestead), Wakefield (Washington's Birthplace), Yeocomico Church.

Level.

Wise County, southwest

Big Stone Gap.

Scenic Roads and Streams.

Wythe County, southwest

Apple Blossoms, Cottages, New River, River Gorge.

Rolling and mountainous.

York County, southeast of Richmond

Old Church (York), *Old Custom House (York), Oldest House in Yorktown, *Moore House (Place of Surrender), Nelson House (York Hall), *Ancient Tavern.